IRISH
SCALAWAGS AND
SCOUNDRELS

IRISH
SCALAWAGS AND
SCOUNDRELS

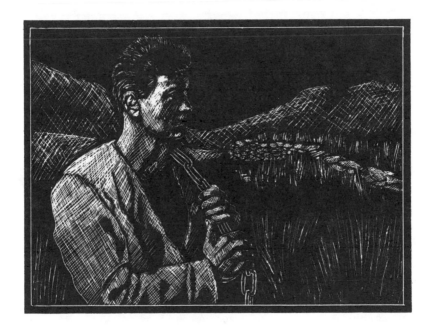

Edited by Mairtin O'Griofa
Illustrated by Sheila Kern

Sterling Publishing Co., Inc.   New York
A STERLING/MAIN STREET BOOK

Designed by John Murphy
Assisted by Edmond Smith
Typeset by Upper Case Limited, Cork, Ireland.

10   9   8   7   6   5   4   3   2   1

A Sterling/Main Street Book

Published in 1996 by Sterling Publishing Company, Inc.
387 Park Avenue South, New York, N.Y. 10016
© 1996 by Sterling Publishing Company, Inc.
Distributed in Canada by Sterling Publishing
% Canadian Manda Group, One Atlantic Avenue, Suite 105
Toronto, Ontario, Canada M6K 3E7
Distributed in Great Britain and Europe by Cassell PLC
Wellington House, 125 Strand, London WC2R 0BB, England
Distributed in Australia by Capricorn Link (Australia) Pty Ltd.
P.O. Box 6651, Baulkham Hills, Business Centre, NSW 2153,
Australia

ISBN 0-8069-5963-0

Contents

Introduction

"SCOUNDRELS"—and "scalawags," its North American equiva-
lent—is one of those wonderful English words with a variety of
ethical and moral meanings. A scoundrel can be both an unprin-
cipled and dishonest person or someone who is playfully mischievous. This collection of nine brilliant stories, both comic and
tragic, contains examples of both types—but with an Irish difference, a Celtic lowest common denominator called "cuteness." In
Ireland, someone who is "cute" is not necessarily, in the
American sense, physically attractive. He or she is clever, canny,
shrewd—for "cute" is short for "acute," and the cute Irish
scoundrel always defeats his antagonists. In the tales that follow,
the truly villainous scoundrels will earn their just deserts, but the
cute scalawag will literally get away with murder.

In *Irish Scalawags and Scoundrels* the Devil makes an
almost fatal mistake when he attempts to claim the soul of one of
the most notorious scoundrels in Ireland; a cute shepherd out-
smarts a tyrannous political official, destroying him and an entire
town in a flood of cataclysmic proportions; an oafish giant of a
man is beaten in a battle of wits and brawn by his feisty but
diminutive half-brother; an entire town of Munster rogues smug-
gles to safety in a Cork pub hundreds of kegs of rum—right
under the noses of constables and magistrates; an experienced
revenue agent attempts to capture a gang of illegal whiskey distillers and fails in a hilarious turn of events; an Irish rascal con-
vinces Satan to build him a mill that mints money; an impover-

7

ished man lies his way to free passage to Canada, only to discover that he needs even more native cuteness to escape from the consequences of those lies; and a scalawag bewitches a fiddle that, in the hands of a born-again Christian musician, causes chaos at a religious revival meeting. And in two totally unconventional tales, we learn the story of a returning Irishman who has struck it rich in America and has the tables turned on him by the fair colleen he abandoned in the Ould Country—and encounter the political allegory, written by the editor of the old Sinn Fein magazine, which shows that what was true a century ago is still true today.

Included among the distinguished Irish writers in this collection are William Carleton (1794-1869); Edith Somerville (1858-1949) and Violet Florence Martin (1862-1915), cousins who wrote under the name of Somerville and Ross; Seamus MacManus (1869-1960); Samual Lover (1797-1868); Shan F. Bullock (1865-1935); and Seamus O'Kely (1875-1918).

Irish Scalawags and Scoundrels will leave you laughing with glee as the cuteness of some Irish rogues save them from the consequences of their hilarious antisocial acts—or have you clutching your hearts as the most monstrous villans suffer horribly for their sins.

The Three Wishes
William Carleton

IN ANCIENT TIMES there lived a man called Billy Dawson, and he was known to be a great rogue. They say he was descended from the family of the Dawsons, which was the reason, I suppose, of his carrying their name upon him.

Billy, in his youthful days, was the best hand at doing nothing in all Europe; devil a mortal could come next or near him at idleness; and, in consequence of his great practice that way, you may be sure that if any man could make a fortune by it he would have done it.

Billy was the only son of his father, barring two daughters, but they have nothing to do with the story I'm telling you. Indeed it was kind father and grandfather for Billy to be handy at the knavery as well as at the idleness, for it was well known that not one of their blood ever did an honest act, except with a roguish intention. In short, they were altogether a *dacent* connection and a credit to the name. As for Billy, all the villainy of the family, both plain and ornamental, came down to him by way of legacy, for it so happened that the father, in spite of all his cleverness, had nothing but his roguery to *lave* him.

Billy, to do him justice, improved the fortune he got. Every day advanced him farther into dishonesty and poverty, until, at the long run, he was acknowledged on all hands to be the completest swindler and the poorest vagabond in the whole parish.

Billy's father, in his young days, had often been forced to acknowledge the inconvenience of not having a trade, in consequence of some nice point in law, called the "Vagrant Act," that sometimes troubled him. On this account he made up his mind to give Bill an occupation, and he accordingly bound him to a blacksmith; but whether Bill was to *live* or *die* by *forgery* was a puzzle to his father—though the neighbors said that *both* was most likely. At all events, he was put apprentice to a smith for seven years, and a hard card his master had to play in managing him. He took the proper method, however, for Bill was so lazy and roguish that it would vex a saint to keep him in order.

"Bill," says his master to him one day that he had been sunning

9

himself about the ditches, instead of minding his business, "Bill, my boy, I'm vexed to the heart to see you in such a bad state of health. You're very ill with that complaint called an *all-overness*; however," says he, "I think I can cure you. Nothing will bring you about but three or four sound doses every day of a medicine called 'the oil o' the hazel.' Take the first dose now," says he, and he immediately banged him with a hazel cudgel until Bill's bones ached for a week afterward.

"If you were my son," said his master, "I tell you that, as long as I could get a piece of advice growing convenient in the hedges, I'd have you a different youth from what you are. If working was a sin, Bill, not an innocenter boy ever broke bread than you would be. Good people's scarce, you think; but however that may be, I throw it out as a hint, that you must take your medicine till you're cured, whenever you happen to get unwell in the same way."

From this out he kept Bill's nose to the grinding stone, and whenever his complaint returned he never failed to give him a hearty dose for his improvement.

In the course of time, however, Bill was his own man and his own master, but it would puzzle a saint to know whether the master or the man was the more precious youth in the eyes of the world.

He immediately married a wife, and devil a doubt of it, but if *he* kept *her* in whisky and sugar, *she* kept *him* in hot water. Bill drank and she drank; Bill fought and she fought; Bill was idle and she was idle; Bill whacked her and she whacked Bill. If Bill gave her one black eye, she gave him another, *just to keep herself in countenance*. Never was there a blessed pair so well met, and a beautiful sight it was to see them both at breakfast time, blinking at each other across the potato basket, Bill with his right eye black, and she with her left.

In short, they were the talk of the whole town; and to see Bill of a morning staggering home drunk, his shirt sleeves rolled up on his smutted arms, his breast open, and an old tattered leather apron, with one corner tucked up under his belt, singing one minute and fighting with his wife the next—she, reeling beside him with a discolored eye, as aforesaid, a dirty ragged cap on one side of her head, a pair of Bill's old slippers on her feet, a squalling child on her arm—now cuffing and dragging Bill, and again kissing and hugging him! Yes, it was a pleasant picture to see this loving pair in such a state!

This might do for a while, but it could not last. They were idle, drunken, and ill conducted; and it was not to be supposed that they would get a farthing candle on their words. They were, of course, *druv* to great straits; and faith, they soon found that their fighting and drinking and idleness made them the laughing sport of the neighbors; but neither brought food to their *childhre*, put a coat upon their backs, nor satisfied their landlord when he came to look for his own. Still, the never a one of Bill but was a funny fellow with strangers, though, as we said, the greatest rogue unhanged.

One day he was standing against his own anvil, completely in a brown study—being brought to his wit's end how to make out a breakfast for the family. The wife was scolding and cursing in the house, and the naked creatures of children squalling about her knees for food. Bill was fairly at an amplush, and knew not where or how to turn himself, when a poor, withered old beggar came into the forge, tottering on his staff. A long white beard fell from his chin, and he looked as thin and hungry that you might blow him, one would think, over the house. Bill at this moment had been brought to his senses by distress, and his heart had a touch of pity toward the old man, for, on looking at him a second time, he clearly saw starvation and sorrow in his face.

"God save you, honest man!" said Bill.

The old man gave a sigh, and raising himself with great pain on his staff, he looked at Bill in a very beseeching way.

"Musha, God save you kindly!" says he. "Maybe you could give a poor, hungry, helpless ould man a mouthful of something to ait? You see yourself I'm not able to work; if I was, I'd scorn to be beholding to anyone."

"Faith, honest man," said Bill, "if you knew who you're speaking to, you'd as soon ask a monkey for a churnstaff as me for either mate or money. There's not a blackguard in the three kingdoms so fairly on the *shaughran* as I am for both the one and the other. The wife within is sending the curses thick and heavy on me, and the *childhre's* playing the cat's melody to keep her in comfort. Take my word for it, poor man, if I had either mate or money I'd help you, for I know particularly well what it is to want them at the present speaking; an empty sack won't stand, neighbor."

So far Bill told him truth. The good thought was in his heart, because he found himself on a footing with the beggar; and nothing brings down pride, or softens the heart, like feeling what it is to want.

"Why, you arc in a worse state than I am," said the old man; "you have a family to provide for, and I have only myself to support."

"You may kiss the book on that, my old worthy," replied Bill; "but come, what I can do for you I will; plant yourself up here beside the fire, and I'll give it a blast or two of my bellows that will warm the old blood in your body. It's a cold, miserable, snowy day, and a good heat will be of service."

"Thank you kindly," said the old man; "I *am* cold, and a warming at your fire will do me good, sure enough. Oh, but it *is* a bitter, bitter day; God bless it!"

He then sat down, and Bill blew a rousing blast that soon made the stranger edge back from the heat. In a short time he felt quite comfortable, and when the numbness was taken out of his joints, he buttoned himself up and prepared to depart.

"Now," says he to Bill, "you hadn't the food to give me, but *what you could you did*. Ask any three wishes you choose, and be they what they may, take my word for it, they shall be granted."

Now, the truth is, that Bill, though he believed himself a great man in point of 'cuteness, wanted, after all, a full quarter of being square, for there is always a great difference between a wise man and a knave. Bill was so much of a rogue that he could not, for the blood of him, ask an honest wish, but stood scratching his head in a puzzle.

"Three wishes!" said he. "Why, let me see—did you say *three*?"

"Ay," replied the stranger, "three wishes—that was what I said."

"Well," said Bill, "here goes—aha!—let me alone, my old worthy!—faith I'll overreach the parish, if what you say is true. I'll cheat them in dozens, rich and poor, old and young; let me alone, man—I have it here," and he tapped his forehead with great glee. "Faith, you're the sort to meet of a frosty morning, when a man wants his breakfast; and I'm sorry that I have neither money nor credit to get a bottle of whisky, that we might take our morning together."

"Well, but let us hear the wishes," said the old man; "my time is short, and I cannot stay much longer."

"Do you see this sledge hammer?" said Bill. "I wish, in the first place, that whoever takes it up in their hands may never be able to lay it down till I give them lave; and that whoever begins to sledge with it may never stop sledging till it's my pleasure to release him.

"Secondly—I have an armchair, and I wish that whoever sits down in it may never rise out of it till they have my consent.

"And, thirdly—that whatever money I put into my purse, nobody may have power to take it out of it but myself!"

"You Devil's rip!" says the old man in a passion, shaking his staff across Bill's nose. "Why did you not ask something that would sarve you both here and hereafter? Sure it's as common as the market cross, that there's not a vagabone in His Majesty's dominions stands more in need of both."

"Oh! By the elevens," said Bill, "I forgot that altogether! Maybe you'd be civil enough to let me change one of them? The sorra purtier wish ever was made than I'll make, if only you'll give me another chance at it."

"Get out, you reprobate," said the old fellow, still in a passion. "Your day of grace is past. Little you knew who was speaking to you all this time. I'm St. Moroky, you blackguard, and I gave you an opportunity of doing something for yourself and your family; but you neglected it, and now your fate is cast, you dirty, bog-trotting profligate. Sure, it's well known what you are! Aren't you a byword in everybody's mouth, you and your scold of a wife? By this and by that, if ever you happen to come across me again, I'll send you to where you won't freeze, you villain!"

He then gave Bill a rap of his cudgel over the head and laid him at his length beside the bellows, kicked a broken coal scuttle out of his way, and left the forge in a fury.

When Billy recovered himself from the effects of the blow and began to think on what had happened, he could have quartered himself with vexation for not asking great wealth as one of the wishes at least; but now the die was cast on him, and he could only make the most of the three he pitched upon.

He now bethought him how he might turn them to the best account, and here his cunning came to his aid. He began by sending for his wealthiest neighbors on pretence of business, and when he got them under his roof he offered them the armchair to sit down in. He now had them safe, nor could all the art of man relieve them except worthy Bill was willing. Bill's plan was to make the best bargain he could before he released his prisoners; and let him alone for knowing how to make their purses bleed. There wasn't a wealthy man in the country he did not fleece. The parson of the parish bled heavily; so did the lawyer; and a rich attorney, who had retired from practice, swore that the Court of Chancery itself was paradise compared to Bill's chair.

This was all very good for a time. The fame of his chair, however, soon spread; so did that of his sledge. In a short time neither man, woman, nor child would darken his door; all avoided him and his fixtures as they would a spring gun or mantrap. Bill, so long as he fleeced his neighbors, never wrought a hand's turn; so that when his money was out he found himself as badly off as ever. In addition to all this, his character was fifty times worse than before, for it was the general belief that he had dealings with the old boy. Nothing now could exceed his misery, distress, and ill temper. The wife and he and their children all fought among one another. Everybody hated them, cursed them, and avoided them. The people thought they were acquainted with more than Christian people ought to know. This, of course, came to Bill's ears, and it vexed him very much.

One day he was walking about the fields, thinking of how he could raise the wind once more; the day was dark, and he found himself, before he stopped, in the bottom of a lonely glen covered by great bushes that grew on each side. "Well," thought he, when every other means of raising money failed him, "it's reported that I'm in league with the old boy, and as it's a folly to have the name of the connection without the profit, I'm ready to make a bargain with him any day—so," said he, raising his voice, "Nick, you sinner, if you be convanient and willing why stand out here; show your best leg—here's your man."

The words were hardly out of his mouth when a dark, sober-looking old gentleman, not unlike a lawyer, walked up to him. Bill looked at the foot and saw the hoof. "Morrow, Nick," says Bill.

"Morrow, Bill," says Nick. "Well, Bill, what's the news?"

"Devil a much myself hears of late," says Bill; "is there anything *fresh* below?"

"I can't exactly say, Bill; I spend little of my time down now; the

Tories are in office, and my hands are consequently too full of business here to pay much attention to anything else."

"A fine place this, sir," says Bill, "to take a constitutional walk in; when I want an appetite I often come this way myself—hem! *High* feeding is very bad without exercise."

"High feeding! Come, come, Bill, you know you didn't taste a morsel these four-and-twenty hours."

"You know that's a bounce, Nick. I ate a breakfast this morning that would put a stone of flesh on you, if you only smelt at it."

"No matter; this is not to the purpose. What's that you were muttering to yourself a while ago? If you want to come to the brunt, here I'm for you."

"Nick," said Bill, "you're complate; you want nothing barring a pair of Brian O'Lynn's breeches."

Bill, in fact, was bent on making his companion open the bargain, because he had often heard that, in that case, with proper care on his own part, he might defeat him in the long run. The other, however, was his match.

"What was the nature of Brian's garment?" inquired Nick.

"Why, you know the song," said Bill:

Brian O'Lynn had no breeches to wear,
So he got a sheep's skin for to make him a pair;
With the fleshy side out and the wooly side in,
'They'll be pleasant and cool,' says Brian O'Lynn.

"A cool pare would sarve you, Nick."

"You're mighty waggish today, Misther Dawson."

"And good right I have," said Bill; "I'm a man snug and well to do in the world; have lots of money, plenty of good eating and drinking, and what more need a man wish for?"

"True," said the other; "in the meantime it's rather odd that so respectable a man should not have six inches of unbroken cloth in his apparel. You're as naked a tatterdemalion as I ever laid my eyes on; in full dress for a party of scarecrows, William?"

"That's my own fancy, Nick; I don't work at my trade like a gentleman. This is my forge dress, you know."

"Well, but what did you summon me here for?" said the other; "you may as well speak out, I tell you, for, my good friend, unless you do, I shan't. Smell that."

"I smell more than that," said Bill; "and by the way, I'll thank you to give me the windy side of you—curse all sulphur, I say. There, that's what I call an improvement in my condition. But as you *are* so stiff," says Bill, "why, the short and long of it is—that—ahem—you see I'm—tut—sure you know I have a thriving trade of my own, and that if I like I needn't be at a loss; but in the meantime I'm rather in a kind of a so—so—don't you *take*?"

And Bill winked knowingly, hoping to trick him into the first proposal.

"You must speak aboveboard, my friend," says the other. "I'm a man of few words, blunt and honest. If you have anything to say, be plain. Don't think I can be losing my time with such a pitiful rascal as you are."

"Well," says Bill. "I want money, then, and am ready to come into terms. What have you to say to that, Nick?"

"Let me see—let me look at you," says his companion, turning him about. "Now, Bill, in the first place, are you not as finished a scarecrow as ever stood upon two legs?"

"I play second fiddle to you there again," says Bill.

"There you stand, with the blackguards' coat of arms quartered under your eye, and—"

"Don't make little of *black*guards," said Bill, "nor spake disparagingly of your *own* crest."

"Why, what would you bring, you brazen rascal, if you were fairly put up at auction?"

"Faith, I'd bring more bidders than you would," said Bill, "if you were to go off at auction tomorrow. I tell you they should bid *downward* to come to your value, Nicholas. We have no coin *small* enough to purchase you."

"Well, no matter," said Nick. "If you are willing to be mine at the expiration of seven years, I will give you more money than ever the rascally breed of you was worth."

"Done!" said Bill. "But no disparagement to my family, in the meantime; so down with the hard cash, and don't be a *neger*."

The money was accordingly paid down; but as nobody was present, except the giver and receiver, the amount of what Bill got was never known.

"Won't you give me a luck penny?" said the old gentleman.

"Tut," said Billy, "so prosperous an old fellow as you cannot want it; however, bad luck to you, with all my heart! and it's rubbing grease to a fat pig to say so. Be off now, or I'll commit suicide on you. Your absence is a cordial to most people, you infernal old profligate. You have injured my morals even for the short time you have been with me, for I don't find myself so virtuous as I was."

"Is that your gratitude, Billy?"

"Is it gratitude *you* speak of, man? I wonder you don't blush when you name it. However, when you come again, if you bring a third eye in your head you will see what I mane, Nicholas, *ahagur*."

The old gentleman, as Bill spoke, hopped across the ditch on his way to *Downing* Street, where of late 'tis thought he possesses much influence.

Bill now began by degrees to show off, but still wrought a little at his trade to blindfold the neighbors. In a very short time, however, he became a great man. So long indeed as he was a poor rascal, no decent person would speak to him; even the proud servingmen at the "Big House" would turn up their noses at him. And he well deserved to be made little of by others, because he was mean enough to make little of himself. But when it was seen and known that he had oceans of money, it was wonderful to think, although he was *now* a greater blackguard than ever, how those who despised him before began to come round him and court his company. Bill, however, had neither sense nor spirit to make those sunshiny friends know their distance; not he—instead of that he was proud to be seen in decent company, and so long as the money lasted, it was "hail fellow well met" between himself and every fair-faced *spunger* who had a horse under him, a decent coat to his back, and a good appetite to eat his dinners. With riches and all, Bill was the same man still; but, somehow or other, there is a great difference between a rich profligate and a poor one, and Bill found it so to his cost in *both* cases.

Before half the seven years was passed, Bill had his carriage and his equipages; was hand and glove with my Lord This, and my Lord That; kept hounds and hunters; was the first sportsman at the Curragh; patronized every boxing ruffian he could pick up; and betted night and day on cards, dice, and horses. Bill, in short, *should* be a blood, and except he did all this, he could not presume to mingle with the fashionable bloods of his time.

It's an old proverb, however, that "what is got over the Devil's back is sure to go off under it," and in Bill's case this proved true. In short, the old boy himself could not supply him with money so fast as he made it fly; it was "come easy, go easy," with Bill, and so sign was on it, before he came within two years of his time he found his purse empty.

And now came the value of his summer friends to be known. When it was discovered that the cash was no longer flush with him—that stud, and carriage, and hounds were going to the hammer—whish! off they went, friends, relations, pot companions, dinner eaters, black-legs, and all, like a flock of crows that had smelled gunpowder. Down Bill soon went, week after week and day after day, until at last he was obliged to put on the leather apron and take to the hammer again; and not only that, for as no experience could make him wise, he once more began his taproom brawls, his quarrels with Judy, and took to his "high feeding" at the dry potatoes and salt. Now, too, came the cutting tongues of all who knew him, like razors upon him. Those that he scorned because they were poor and himself rich now paid him back his own with interest; and those that he had measured himself with, because they were rich, and who only countenanced him in consequence of his wealth, gave him the hardest word in their cheeks. The Devil mend him! He deserved it all, and more if he had got it.

Bill, however, who was a hardened sinner, never fretted himself down an ounce of flesh by what was said to him or of him. Not he; he cursed, and fought, and swore, and schemed away as usual, taking in everyone he could; and surely none could match him at villainy of all sorts and sizes.

At last the seven years became expired, and Bill was one morning sitting in his forge, sober and hungry, the wife cursing him, and the children squalling as before; he was thinking how he might defraud some honest neighbor out of a breakfast to stop their mouths and his own, too, when who walks in to him but old Nick to demand his bargain.

"Morrow, Bill!" says he with a sneer.

"The Devil welcome you!" says Bill. "But you have a fresh memory."

"A bargain's a bargain between two *honest* men, any day," says Satan; "when I speak of honest men, I mean yourself and *me*, Bill"; and he put his tongue in his cheek to make game of the unfortunate rogue he had come for.

"Nick, my worthy fellow," said Bill, "have bowels; you wouldn't do a shabby thing; you wouldn't disgrace your own character by putting more weight upon a falling man. You know what it is to get a *comedown* yourself, my worthy; so just keep your toe in your pump, and walk off with yourself somewhere else. A *cool* walk will sarve you better than my company, Nicholas."

"Bill, it's no use in shirking," said his friend; "your swindling tricks may enable you to cheat others, but you won't cheat *me*, I guess. You want nothing to make you perfect in your way but to travel; and travel you shall under my guidance, Billy. No, no—I'm not to be swindled, my good fellow. I have rather a—a—better opinion of myself, Mr. D., than to think that you could outwit one Nicholas Clutie, Esq.—ahem!"

"You may sneer, you sinner," replied Bill, "but I tell you that I have outwitted men who could buy and sell you to your face. Despair, you villain, when I tell you that *no attorney* could stand before me."

Satan's countenance got blank when he heard this; he wriggled and fidgeted about and appeared to be not quite comfortable.

"In that case, then," says he, "the sooner I *deceive* you the better; so turn out for the *Low Countries*."

"Is it come to that in earnest?" said Bill. "And are you going to act the rascal at the long run?"

"'Pon honor, Bill."

"Have patience, then, you sinner, till I finish this horseshoe—it's the last of a set I'm finishing for one of your friend the attorney's horses. And here, Nick, I hate idleness; you know it's the mother of mischief; take this sledge hammer and give a dozen strokes or so, till I get it out of hands, and then here's with you, since it must be so."

He then gave the bellows a puff that blew half a peck of dust in Clubfoot's face, whipped out the red-hot iron, and set Satan sledging away for bare life.

"Faith," says Bill to him, when the shoe was finished, "it's a thousand pities ever the sledge should be out of your hand; the great *Parra Gow* was a child to you at sledging, you're such an able tyke.

Now just exercise yourself till I bid the wife and *childhre* good-by, and then I'm off."

Out went Bill, of course, without the slightest notion of coming back; no more than Nick had that he could not give up the sledging, and indeed neither could he, but was forced to work away as if he was sledging for a wager. This was just what Bill wanted. He was now compelled to sledge on until it was Bill's pleasure to release him; and so we leave him very industriously employed, while we look after the worthy who outwitted him.

In the meantime Bill broke cover and took to the country at large; wrought a little journey work wherever he could get it, and in this way went from one place to another, till, in the course of a month, he walked back very coolly into his own forge to see how things went on in his absence. There he found Satan in a rage, the perspiration pouring from him in torrents, hammering with might and main upon the naked anvil. Bill calmly leaned back against the wall, placed his hat upon the side of his head, put his hands into his breeches pockets, and began to whistle *Shaun Gow's* hornpipe. At length he says, in a very quiet and good-humored way:

"Morrow, Nick!"

"Oh!" says Nick, still hammering away. "Oh! you double-distilled villain (hech!), may the most refined ornamental (hech!) collection of curses that ever was gathered (hech!) into a single nosegay of ill fortune (hech!) shine in the buttonhole of your conscience (hech!) while your name is Bill Dawson! I denounce you (hech!) as a doublemilled villain, a finished, hot-pressed knave (hech!), in comparison of whom all the other knaves I ever knew (hech!), attorneys included, are honest men. I brand you (hech!) as the pearl of cheats, a tiptop take-in (hech!). I denounce you, I say again, for the villainous treatment (hech!) I have received at your hands in this most untoward (hech!) and unfortunate transaction between us; for (hech!) unfortunate, in every sense, is he that has anything to do with (hech!) such a prime and finished impostor."

"You're very warm, Nicky," says Bill; "what puts you into a passion, you old sinner? Sure if it's your own will and pleasure to take exercise at my anvil, *I'm* not to be abused for it. Upon my credit, Nicky, you ought to blush for using such blackguard language, so unbecoming your grave character. You cannot say that it was I set you a-hammering at the empty anvil, you profligate.

"However, as you are so very industrious, I simply say it would be a thousand pities to take you from it. Nick, I love industry in my heart, and I always encourage it, so work away; it's not often you spend your time so creditably. I'm afraid if you weren't at that you'd be worse employed."

"Bill, have bowels," said the operative; "you wouldn't go to lay more weight on a falling man, you know; you wouldn't disgrace your character by such a piece of iniquity as keeping an inoffensive gentleman advanced in years, at such an unbecoming and rascally job as this. Generosity's your top virtue, Bill; not but that you have many other excellent ones, as well as that, among which, as you say yourself, I reckon industry; but still it is in generosity you shine. Come, Bill, honor bright, and release me."

"Name the terms, you profligate."

"You're above terms, William; a generous fellow like you never thinks of terms."

"Good-by, old gentleman!" said Bill very coolly. "I'll drop in to see you once a month."

"No, no, Bill, you infern—a—a—. You excellent, worthy, delightful fellow, not so fast; not so fast. Come, name your terms, you sland— My dear Bill, name your terms."

"Seven years more."

"I agree; but—"

"And the same supply of cash as before, down on the nail here."

"Very good; very good. You're rather simple, Bill; rather soft, I must confess. Well, no matter. I shall yet turn the tab—a—hem! You are an exceedingly simple fellow, Bill; still there will come a day, my *dear* Bill—there will come—'

"Do you grumble, you vagrant? Another word, and I double the terms."

"Mum, William—mum; *tace* is Latin for a candle."

"Seven years more of grace, and the same measure of the needful that I got before. Ay or no?"

"Of grace, Bill! Ay! Ay! Ay! There's the cash. I accept the terms. Oh, blood! The rascal—of grace! Bill!"

"Well, now drop the hammer and vanish," says Billy; "but what would you think to take this sledge, while you stay, and give me a— Eh! Why in such a hurry?" he added, seeing that Satan withdrew in double-quick time.

"Hello! Nicholas!" he shouted. "Come back; you forgot something!" And when the old gentleman looked behind him, Billy shook the hammer at him, on which he vanished altogether.

Billy now got into his old courses; and what shows the kind of people the world is made of, he also took up with his old company. When they saw that he had the money once more and was sowing it about him in all directions, they immediately began to find excuses for his former extravagance.

"Say what you will," said one, "Bill Dawson's a spirited fellow that bleeds like a prince."

"He's a hospitable man in his own house, or out of it, as ever lived," said another.

"His only fault is," observed a third, "that he is, if anything, too generous and doesn't know the value of money; his fault's on the right side, however."

"He has the spunk in him," said a fourth; "keeps a capital table, prime wines, and a standing welcome for his friends."

"Why," said a fifth, "if he doesn't enjoy his money while he lives, he won't when he's dead; so more power to him, and a wider throat to his purse."

Indeed, the very persons who were cramming themselves at his expense despised him at heart. They knew very well, however, how to take him on the weak side. Praise his generosity, and he would do anything; call him a man of spirit, and you might fleece him to his face. Sometimes he would toss a purse of guineas to this knave, another to that flatterer, a third to a bully, and a fourth to some broken-down rake—and all to convince them that he was a sterling friend—a man of mettle and liberality. But never was he known to help a virtuous and struggling family—to assist the widow or the fatherless, or to do any other act that was truly useful. It is to be supposed the reason of this was that as he spent it, as most of the world do, in the service of the Devil, by whose aid he got it, he was prevented from turning it to a good account. Between you and me, dear reader, there are more persons acting after Bill's fashion in the same world than you dream about.

When his money was out again, his friends played him the same rascally game once more. No sooner did his poverty become plain than the knaves began to be troubled with small fits of modesty, such as an unwillingness to come to his place when there was no longer anything to be got there. A kind of virgin bashfulness prevented them from speaking to him when they saw him getting out on the wrong side of his clothes. Many of them would turn away from him in the prettiest and most delicate manner when they thought he wanted to borrow money from them—all for fear of putting him to the blush for asking it. Others again, when they saw him coming toward their houses about dinner hour, would become so confused, from mere gratitude, as to think themselves in another place; and their servants, seized, as it were, with the same feeling, would tell Bill that their masters were "not at home."

At length, after traveling the same villainous round as before, Bill was compelled to betake himself, as the last remedy, to the forge; in other words, he found that there is, after all, nothing in this world that a man can rely on so firmly and surely as his own industry. Bill, however, wanted the organ of common sense, for his experience—and it was sharp enough to leave an impression—ran off him like water off a duck.

He took to his employment sorely against his grain, but he had now no choice. He must either work or starve, and starvation is like a great doctor—nobody tries it till every other remedy fails them. Bill had been twice rich; twice a gentleman among blackguards, but always a blackguard among gentlemen, for no wealth or acquaintance with decent society could rub the rust of his native vulgarity off him. He was now a common blinking sot in his forge; a drunken bully in the taproom, cursing and browbeating everyone as well as his wife; boasting of how much money he had spent in his day; swaggering about the high doings he carried on; telling stories about himself and Lord This at the Curragh; the dinners he gave—how much they cost him—and attempting to extort credit upon the strength of his former wealth. He was too ignorant, however, to know that he was publishing his own disgrace and that it was a mean-spirited thing to be proud of what ought to make him blush through a deal board nine inches thick.

He was one morning industriously engaged in a quarrel with his wife, who, with a three-legged stool in her hand, appeared to mistake his head for his own anvil; he, in the meantime, paid his addresses to her with his leather apron, when who steps in to jog his memory about the little agreement that was between them but old Nick. The wife, it seems, in spite of all her exertions to the contrary, was getting the worst of it; and Sir Nicholas, willing to appear a gentleman of great gallantry, thought he could not do less than take up the lady's quarrel, particularly as Bill had laid her in a sleeping posture. Now Satan thought this too bad, and as he felt himself under many obligations to the sex, he determined to defend one of them on the present occasion; so as Judy rose, he turned upon her husband and floored him by a clever facer.

"You unmanly villain," said he, "is this the way you treat your wife? 'Pon honor Bill, I'll chastise you on the spot. I could not stand by, a spectator of such ungentlemanly conduct, without giving you all claim to gallant—" Whack! The word was divided in his mouth by the blow of a churnstaff from Judy, who no sooner saw Bill struck than she nailed Satan, who "fell" once more.

"What, you villain! That's for striking my husband like a murderer behind his back," said Judy, and she suited the action to the word. "That's for interfering between man and wife. Would you murder the poor man before my face, eh? If he bates me, you shabby dog you, who has a better right? I'm sure it's nothing out of your pocket. Must you have your finger in every pie?"

This was anything but *idle* talk, for at every word she gave him a remembrance, hot and heavy. Nicholas backed, danced, and hopped; she advanced, still drubbing him with great perseverance, till at length he fell into the redoubtable armchair, which stood exactly behind him. Bill, who had been putting in two blows for Judy's one, seeing that his enemy was safe, now got between the Devil and his wife, *a situation that few will be disposed to envy him.*

"Tenderness, Judy," said the husband; "I hate cruelty. Go put the tongs in the fire, and make them red-hot. Nicholas, you have a nose," said he.

Satan began to rise but was rather surprised to find that he could not budge.

"Nicholas," says Bill, "how is your pulse? You don't look well; that is to say, you look worse than usual."

The other attempted to rise but found it a mistake.

"I'll thank you to come along," said Bill. "I have a fancy to travel under your guidance, and we'll take the *Low Countries* in our way, won't we? Get to your legs, you sinner; you know a bargain's a bargain between two *honest* men, Nicholas, meaning *yourself* and *me*. Judy, are the tongs hot?"

Satan's face was worth looking at as he turned his eyes from the husband to the wife and then fastened them on the tongs, now nearly at a furnace heat in the fire, conscious at the same time that he could not move out of the chair.

"Billy," said he, "you won't forget that I rewarded you generously the last time I saw you, in the way of business."

"Faith, Nicholas, it fails me to remember any generosity I ever showed you. Don't be womanish. I simply want to see what kind of stuff your nose is made of and whether it will stretch like a rogue's conscience. If it does we will flatter it up the chimly with red-hot tongs, and when this old hat is fixed on the top of it, let us alone for a weathercock."

"Have a *fellow feeling*, Mr. Dawson; you know we ought not to dispute. Drop the matter, and I give you the next seven years."

"We know all that," says Billy, opening the red-hot tongs very coolly.

"Mr. Dawson," said Satan, "if you cannot remember my friendship to yourself, don't forget how often I stood your father's friend, your grandfather's friend, and the friend of all your relations up to the tenth generation. I intended, also, to stand by your children after you, so long as the name of Dawson—and a respectable one it is—might last."

"Don't be blushing, Nick," says Bill; "you are too modest; that was ever your failing; hold up your head, there's money bid for you. I'll give you such a nose, my good friend, that you will have to keep an outrider before you, to carry the end of it on his shoulder."

"Mr. Dawson, I pledge my honor to raise your children in the world as high as they can go, no matter whether they desire it or not."

"That's very kind of you," says the other, "and I'll do as much for your nose."

He gripped it as he spoke, and the old boy immediately sung out; Bill pulled, and the nose went with him like a piece of warm wax. He then transferred the tongs to Judy, got a ladder, resumed the tongs, ascended the chimney, and tugged stoutly at the nose until he got it five feet above the roof. He then fixed the hat upon the top of it and came down.

"There's a weathercock," said Billy; "I defy Ireland to show such a beauty. Faith, Nick, it would make the purtiest steeple for a church in all Europe, and the old hat fits it to a shaving."

In this state, with his nose twisted up the chimney, Satan sat for some time, experiencing the novelty of what might be termed a peculiar sensation. At last the worthy husband and wife began to relent.

"I think," said Bill, "that we have made the most of the nose, as well as the joke; I believe, Judy, it's long enough."

"What is?" says Judy.

"Why, the joke," said the husband.

"Faith, and I think so is the nose," said Judy.

"What do you say yourself, Satan?" said Bill.

"Nothing at all, William," said the other; "but that—ha! ha!—it's a good joke—an excellent joke, and a goodly nose, too, as it *stands*. You were always a gentlemanly man, Bill, and did things with a grace; still, if I might give an opinion on such a trifle—"

"It's no trifle at all," says Bill, "if you spake of the nose."

"Very well, it is not," says the other; "still, I am decidedly of opinion that if you could shorten both the joke and the nose without further violence, you would lay me under very heavy obligations, which I shall be ready to acknowledge and *repay* as I ought."

"Come," said Bill, "shell out once more, and be off for seven years. As much as you came down with the last time, and vanish."

The words were scarcely spoken, when the money was at his feet and Satan invisible. Nothing could surpass the mirth of Bill and his wife at the result of this adventure. They laughed till they fell down on the floor.

It is useless to go over the same ground again. Bill was still incorrigible. The money went as the Devil's money always goes. Bill caroused and squandered but could never turn a penny of it to a good purpose. In this way year after year went, till the seventh was closed and Bill's hour come. He was now, and had been for some time past, as miserable a knave as ever. Not a shilling had he, nor a shilling's worth, with the exception of his forge, his cabin, and a few articles of crazy furniture. In this state he was standing in his forge as before, straining his ingenuity how to make out a breakfast, when Satan came to look after him. The old gentleman was sorely puzzled how to get at him. He kept skulking and sneaking about the forge for some time, till he saw that Bill hadn't a cross to bless himself with. He immediately changed himself into a guinea and lay in an open place where he knew Bill would see him. "If," said he, "I once get into his possession, I can manage him." The honest smith took the bait, for it was well gilded; he clutched the guinea, put it into his purse, and closed it up. "Ho! Ho!" shouted the Devil out of the purse. "You're caught, Bill; I've secured you at last, you knave you. Why don't you despair you villain, when you think of what's before you?"

"Why, you unlucky ould dog," said Bill, "is it there you are? Will you always drive your head into every loophole that's set for you? Faith, Nick *achora,* I never had you bagged till now."

Satan then began to tug and struggle with a view of getting out of the purse, but in vain.

"Mr. Dawson," said he, "we understand each other. I'll give the seven years additional and the cash on the nail."

"Be aisey, Nicholas. You know the weight of the hammer, that's enough. It's not a whipping with feathers you're going to get, anyhow. Just be aisey."

"Mr. Dawson, I grant I'm not your match. Release me, and I double the case. I was merely trying your temper when I took the shape of a guinea."

"Faith and I'll try yours before I lave it, I've a notion." He immediately commenced with the sledge, and Satan sang out with a considerable want of firmness. "Am I heavy enough?" said Bill.

"Lighter, lighter, William, if you love me. I haven't been well latterly, Mr. Dawson—I have been delicate—my health, in short, is in a very precarious state, Mr. Dawson."

"I can believe *that*,' said Bill, "and it will be more so before I have done with you. Am I doing it right?"

"Bill," said Nick, "is this gentlemanly treatment in your own respectable shop? Do you think, if you dropped into my little place, that I'd act this rascally part toward you? Have you no compunction?"

"I know," replied Bill, sledging away with vehemence, "that you're notorious for giving your friends a *warm* welcome. Divil an ould youth more so; but you must be daling in bad coin, must you? However, good or bad, you're in for a sweat now, you sinner. Am I doin' it purty?"

"Lovely, William—but, if possible, a little more delicate."

"Oh, how delicate you are! Maybe a cup o' tay would sarve you, or a little small gruel to compose your stomach?"

"Mr. Dawson," said the gentleman in the purse, "hold your hand and let us understand one another. I have a proposal to make."

"Hear the sinner anyhow," said the wife.

"Name your own sum," said Satan, "only set me free."

"No, the sorra may take the toe you'll budge till you let Bill off," said the wife; "hould him hard, Bill, barrin' he sets you clear of your engagement."

"There it is, my posy," said Bill; "that's the condition. If you don't give *me up*, here's at you once more—and you must double the cash you gave the last time, too. So, if you're of that opinion, say *ay*—leave the cash and be off."

The money appeared in a glittering heap before Bill, upon which he exclaimed, "The *ay* has it, you dog. Take to your pumps now, and fair weather after you, you vagrant; but, Nicholas—Nick—here, here—" The other looked back and saw Bill, with a broad grin upon him, shaking the purse at him. "Nicholas, come back," said he. "I'm short a guinea." Nick shook his fist and disappeared.

It would be useless to stop now, merely to inform our readers that Bill was beyond improvement. In short, he once more took to his old habits and lived on exactly in the same manner as before. He had two sons—one as great a blackguard as himself, and who was also named after him; the other was a well-conducted, virtuous young man called James, who left his father and, having relied upon his own industry and honest perseverance in life, arrived afterward to great wealth and built the town called Castle Dawson, which is so called from its founder until this day.

Bill, at length, in spite of all his wealth, was obliged, as he himself said, "to travel"—in other words, he fell asleep one day and forgot to awaken; or, in still plainer terms, he died.

Now, it is usual, when a man dies, to close the history of his life and adventures at once; but with our hero this cannot be the case. The moment Bill departed he very naturally bent his steps toward the residence of St. Moroky, as being, in his opinion, likely to lead him toward the snuggest berth he could readily make out. On arriving, he gave a very humble kind of knock, and St. Moroky appeared.

"God save your Reverence!" said Bill, very submissively.

"Be off; there's no admittance here for so poor a youth as you are," said St. Moroky.

He was now so cold and fatigued that he cared like where he went, provided only, as he said himself, "he could rest his bones and get an air of the fire." Accordingly, after arriving at a large black gate, he knocked, as before, and was told he would get *instant* admittance the moment he gave his name.

"Billy Dawson," he replied.

"Off, instantly," said the porter to his companions, "and let His Majesty know that the rascal he dreads so much is here at the gate."

Such a racket and tumult were never heard as the very mention of Billy Dawson created.

In the meantime, his old acquaintance came running toward the gate with such haste and consternation that his tail was several times nearly tripping up his heels.

"Don't admit that rascal," he shouted; "bar the gate—make every chain and lock and bolt fast—I won't be safe—and I won't stay here, nor none of us need stay here, if he gets in—my bones are sore yet after him. No, no—begone, you villain—you'll get no entrance here— I know you too well."

Bill could not help giving a broad, malicious grin at Satan, and, putting his nose through the bars, he exclaimed, "Ha! You ould dog, I have you afraid of me at last, have I?"

He had scarcely uttered the words, when his foe, who stood inside, instantly tweaked him by the nose, and Bill felt as if he had been gripped by the same red-hot tongs with which he himself had formerly tweaked the nose of Nicholas.

Bill then departed but soon found that in consequence of the inflammable materials which strong drink had thrown into his nose, that organ immediately took fire, and, indeed, to tell the truth, kept burning night and day, winter and summer, without ever once going out from that hour to this.

Such was the sad fate of Billy Dawson, who has been walking without stop or stay, from place to place, ever since; and in consequence of the flame on his nose, and his beard being tangled like a wisp of hay, he has been christened by the country folk Will-o'-the-Wisp, while, as it were, to show the mischief of his disposition, the circulating knave, knowing that he must seek the coldest bogs and quagmires in order to cool his nose, seizes upon that opportunity of misleading the unthinking and tipsy night travelers from their way, just that he may have the satisfaction of still taking in as many as possible.

The Holy Island
Somerville and Ross

FOR THREE DAYS of November a white fog stood motionless over the country. All day and all night smothered booms and bangs away to the south-west told that the Fastnet gun was hard at work, and the sirens of the American liners uplifted their monstrous female voices as they felt their way along the coast of Cork. On the third afternoon the wind began to whine about the windows of Shreelane, and the barometer fell like a stone. At 11 p.m. the storm rushed upon us with the roar and the suddenness of a train; the chimneys bellowed, the tall old house quivered, and the yelling wind drove against it, as a man puts his shoulder against a door to burst it in.

We none of us got much sleep, and if Mrs. Cadogan is to be believed—which experience assured me she is not—she spent the night in devotional exercises, and in ministering to the panic-stricken kitchen-maid by the light of a Blessed candle. All that day the storm screamed on, dry-eyed; at nightfall the rain began, and next morning, which happened to be Sunday, every servant in the house was a messenger of Job, laden with tales of leakages, floods, and fallen trees, and inflated with the ill-concealed glory of their kind in evil tidings. To Peter Cadogan, who had been to early Mass, was reserved the crowning satisfaction of reporting that a big vessel had gone on the rocks at Yokahn Point the evening before, and was breaking up fast; it was rumored that the crew had got ashore, but this feature, being favorable and uninteresting, was kept as much as possible in the background. Mrs. Cadogan, who had been to America in an ocean liner, became at once the latest authority on shipwrecks, and was of opinion that "whoever would be dhrownded, it wouldn't be thim lads o' sailors. Sure wasn't there the greatest storm ever was in it the time meself was on the say, and what'd thim fellows do but to put us below entirely in the ship, and close down the doors on us, the way theirselves'd leg it when we'd be dhrownding!"

This view of the position was so startlingly novel that Philippa withdrew suddenly from the task of ordering dinner, and fell up the kitchen stairs in unsuitable laughter. Philippa has not the most rudimentary capacity for keeping her countenance.

That afternoon I was wrapped in the slumber, balmiest and most profound, that follows on a wet Sunday luncheon, when Murray, our DI of police, drove up in uniform, and came into the house on the top of a gust that set every door banging and every picture dancing on the walls. He looked as if his eyes had been blown out of his head, and he wanted something to eat very badly.

"I've been down at the wreck since ten o'clock this morning," he said, "waiting for her to break up, and once she does there'll be trouble. She's an American ship, and she's full up with rum, and bacon, and butter, and all sorts. Bosanquet is there with all his coastguards, and there are five hundred country people on the strand at this moment, waiting for the fun to begin. I've got ten of my fellows there, and I wish I had as many more. You'd better come back with me, Yeates, we may want the Riot Act before all's done!"

The heavy rain had ceased, but it seemed as if it had fed the wind instead of calming it, and when Murray and I drove out of Shreelane, the whole dirty sky was moving, full sailed, in from the south-west, and the telegraph wires were hanging in a loop from the post outside the gate. Nothing except a Skebawn car-horse would have faced the whooping charges of the wind that came at us across Corran Lake; stimulated mysteriously by whistles from the driver, Murray's yellow hireling pounded woodenly along against the blast, till the smell of the torn sea-weed was borne upon it, and we saw the Atlantic waves come towering into the bay of Tralagough.

The ship was, or had been, a three-masted barque; two of her masts were gone, and her bows stood high out of water on the reef that forms one of the shark-like jaws of the bay. The long strand was crowded with groups of people, from the bank of heavy shingle that had been hurled over on to the road, down to the slope where the waves pitched themselves and climbed and fought and tore the gravel back with them, as though they had dug their fingers in. The people were nearly all men, dressed solemnly and hideously in their Sunday clothes; most of them had come straight from Mass without any dinner, true to that Irish instinct that places its fun before its food. That the wreck was regarded as a spree of the largest kind was sufficiently obvious. Our car pulled up at a public-house that stood askew between the road and the shingle; it was humming with those whom Irish publicans were pleased to call "Bonâ feeds," and sundry of the same class were clustered round the door. Under the wall on the leeside was seated a bagpiper, droning out "The Irish Washerwoman" with nodding head and tapping heel, and a young man was cutting a few steps of a jig for the delectation of a group of girls.

So far Murray's constabulary had done nothing but exhibit their imposing chest measurements and spotless uniforms to the Atlantic, and Bosanquet's coastguards had only salvaged some spars, the debris of a boat, and a dead sheep, but their time was coming. As we stumbled down over the shingle, battered by the wind and pelted by clots of foam, someone beside me shouted, "She's gone!" A hill of water had smothered the wreck, and when it fell from her again nothing was left but the bows, with the bowsprit hanging from them in a tangle of rigging. The clouds, bronzed by an unseen sunset, hung low over her; in that greedy pack of waves, with the remorseless rocks above and below her, she seemed the most lonely and tormented of creatures.

About half-an-hour afterwards the cargo began to come ashore on the top of the rising tide. Barrels were plunging and diving in the trough of the waves, like a school of porpoises; they were pitched up the beach in waist-deep rushes of foam; they rolled down again, and were swung up and shouldered by the next wave, playing a kind of Tom Tiddler's ground with the coastguards. Some of the barrels were big and dangerous, some were small and nimble like young pigs, and the bluejackets were up to their middles as their prey dodged and ducked, and the police lined out along the beach to keep back the people. Ten men of the RIC can do a great deal, but they cannot be in more than twenty or thirty places at the same instant; therefore they could hardly cope with a scattered and extremely active mob of four or five hundred, many of whom had taken advantage of their privileges as "bona-fide travelers," and all of whom were determined on getting at the rum.

As the dusk fell the thing got more and more out of hand; the people had found out that the big puncheons held the rum, and had succeeded in capturing one. In the twinkling of an eye it was broached, and fifty backs were shoving round it like a football scrummage. I

have heard many rows in my time: I have seen two Irish regiments—
one of them Militia—at each other's throats in Fermoy barracks; I
have heard Philippa's water spaniel and two fox-terriers hunting a
strange cat round the dairy; but never have I known such untrammeled
bedlam as that which yelled round the rum-casks on Tralagough
strand. For it was soon not a question of one broached cask, or even of
two. The barrels were coming in fast, so fast that it was impossible for
the representatives of law and order to keep on any sort of terms with
them. The people, shouting with laughter, stove in the casks, and drank
rum at 34° above proof, out of their hands, out of their hats, out of
their boots. Women came fluttering over the hillsides through the
twilight, carrying jugs, milk-pails, anything that would hold the liquor.
I saw one of them, roaring with laughter, tilt a filthy zinc bucket to an
old man's lips.

With the darkness came anarchy. The rising tide brought more and
yet more booty: great spars came lunging in on the lap of the waves,
mixed up with cabin furniture, seaman's chests, and the black and
slippery barrels, and the country people continued to flock in, and the
drinking became more and more unbridled. Murray sent for more men
and a doctor, and we slaved on hopelessly in the dark; collaring half-
drunken men, shoving pig-headed casks up hills of shingle, hustling in
among groups of roaring drinkers—we rescued perhaps one barrel in
half-a-dozen. I began to know that there were men there who were not
drunk and were not idle; I was also aware, as the strenuous hours of
darkness passed, of an occasional rumble of cart wheels on the road. It
was evident that the casks which were broached were the least part of
the looting, but even they were beyond our control. The most that
Bosanquet, Murray, and I could do was to concentrate our forces on
the casks that had been secured, and to organize charges upon the
swilling crowds in order to upset the casks that they had broached.
Already men and boys were lying about, limp as leeches, motionless
as the dead.

"They'll kill themselves before morning, at this rate!" shouted
Murray to me. "They're drinking it by the quart! Here's another barrel;
come on!"

We rallied our small forces, and after a brief but furious struggle
succeeded in capsizing it. It poured away in a flood over the stones,

over the prostrate figures that sprawled on them, and a howl of reproach followed.

"If ye pour away any more o' that, Major," said an unctuous voice in my ear, "ye'll intoxicate the stones and they'll be getting up and knocking us down!"

I had been aware of a fat shoulder next to mine in the throng as we heaved the puncheon over, and I now recognized the ponderous wit and Falstaffian figure of Mr. James Canty, a noted member of the Skebawn Board of Guardians, and the owner of a large farm near at hand.

"I never saw worse work on this strand," he went on, "I considher these debaucheries a disgrace to the counthry."

Mr. Canty was famous as an orator, and I presume that it was from long practice among his fellow PLG's that he was able, without apparent exertion, to out-shout the storm.

At this juncture the long-awaited reinforcements arrived, and along with them came Dr. Jerome Hickey, armed with a black bag. Having mentioned that the bag contained a pump—not one of the common or garden variety—and that no pump on board a foundering ship had more arduous labors to perform, I prefer to pass to other themes. The wreck, which had at first appeared to be as inexhaustible and as variously stocked as that in the *Swiss Family Robinson,* was beginning to fail in its supply. The crowd were by this time for the most part incapable from drink, and the fresh contingent of police tackled their work with some prospect of success by the light of a tar barrel, contributed by the owner of the public-house. At about the same time I began to be aware that I was aching with fatigue, that my clothes hung heavy and soaked upon me, that my face was stiff with the salt spray and the bitter wind, and that it was two hours past dinner-time. The possibility of fried salt herrings and hot whisky and water at the public-house rose dazzlingly before my mind, when Mr. Canty again crossed my path.

"In my opinion ye have the whole cargo under conthrol now, Major," he said, "and the police and the sailors should be able to account for it all now by the help of the light. Wasn't I the finished fool that I didn't think to send up to my house for a tea barrel before now! Well—we're all foolish sometimes! But indeed it's time for us to give over, and that's what I'm after saying to the Captain and Mr. Murray. You're exhausted now the three of ye, and if I might make so bold, I'd suggest that ye'd come up to my little place and have what'd warm ye before ye'd go home. It's only a few perches up the road."

The tide had turned, the rain had begun again, and the tar barrel illuminated the fact that Dr. Hickey's dreadful duties alone were pressing. We held a council and finally followed Mr. Canty, picking our way through wreckage of all kinds, including the human variety. Near the public-house I stumbled over something that was soft and had a squeak in it; it was the piper, with his head and shoulders in an overturned rum-barrel, and the bagpipes still under his arm.

I knew the outward appearance of Mr. Canty's house very well. It was a typical southern farmhouse, with dirty whitewashed walls, a slated roof, and small, hermetically-sealed windows staring at the morass of manure which constituted the yard. We followed Mr. Canty up the filthy lane that led to it, picked our way round vague and squelching spurs of the manure heap, and were finally led through the kitchen into a stifling best parlor. Mrs. Canty, a vast and slatternly matron, had evidently made preparations for us; there was a newly-lighted fire pouring flame up the chimney from layers of bogwood, there were whisky and brandy on the table, and a plateful of biscuits sugared in white and pink. Upon our hostess was a black silk dress which indifferently concealed the fact that she was short of boot-laces, and that the boots themselves had made many excursions to the yard and none to the blacking-bottle. Her manners, however, were admirable, and while I live I shall not forget her potato cakes. They came in hot and hot from a pot-oven, they were speckled with caraway seeds, they swam in salt butter, and we ate them shamelessly and greasily, and washed them down with hot whisky and water; I knew to a nicety how ill I should be next day, and heeded not.

"Well, gentlemen," remarked Mr. Canty later on, in his best Board of Guardians' manners, "I've seen many wrecks between this and the Mizen Head, but I never witnessed a scene of more disgraceful excess than what was in it tonight."

"Hear, hear!" murmured Bosanquet with unseemly levity.

"I should say," went on Mr. Canty, "there was at one time tonight upwards of one hundhred men dead dhrunk on the strand, or anyway so dhrunk that if they'd attempt to spake they'd foam at the mouth."

"The craytures!" interjected Mrs. Canty sympathetically.

"But if they're dhrunk today," continued our host, "it's nothing at all to what they'll be tomorrow and afther tomorrow, and it won't be on the strand they'll be dhrinkin' it."

"Why, where will it be!" said Bosanquet, with his disconcerting English way of asking a point-blank question.

Mr. Canty passed his hand over his red cheeks.

"There'll be plenty asking that before all's said and done, Captain," he said, with a compassionate smile, "and there'll be plenty that could give the answer if they'll like, but by dam I don't think ye'll be apt to get much out of the Yokahn boys!"

"The Lord save us, 'twould be better to keep out from the likes o' thim!" put in Mrs. Canty, sliding a fresh avalanche of potato cakes on to the dish; "didn't they pull the clothes off the gauger and pour potheen down his throath till he ran screeching through the streets o' Skebawn!"

James Canty chuckled.

"I remember there was a wreck here one time, and the undherwriters put me in charge of the cargo. Brandy it was—cases of the best Frinch brandy. The people had a song about it, what's this the first verse was —

> One night to the rocks of Yokahn
> Came the barque *Isabella* so dandy,
> To pieces she went before dawn,
> Herself and her cargo of brandy.
> And all met a wathery grave
> Excepting the vessel's car*pen*ther,
> Poor fellow, so far from his home.

Mr. Canty chanted these touching lines in a tuneful if wheezy tenor. "Well, gentlemen, we'll all friends here," he continued, "and it's no harm to mention that this man below at the public-house came askin' me would I let him have some of it for a consideration. 'Sullivan,' says I to him, 'if ye ran down gold in a cup in place of the brandy, I wouldn't give it to you. Of coorse,' says I, 'I'm not sayin' but that if a bottle was to get a crack of a stick, and it to be broken and a man to drink a glass out of it, that would be no more than an accident.' 'That's no good to me,' says he, 'but if I had twelve gallons of that brandy in Cork,' says he, 'by the Holy German!' says he, saying an awful curse, 'I'll sell twenty-five out of it!' Well, indeed, it was true for him; it was grand stuff. As the saying is, it would make a horse out of a cow!"

"It appears to be a handy sort of place for keeping a pub," said Bosanquet.

"Shut to the door, Margaret," said Mr. Canty with elaborate caution. "It'd be a queer place that wouldn't be handy for Sullivan!"

A further tale of great length was in progress when Dr. Hickey's Mephistophelian nose was poked into the best parlor.

"Hullo, Hickey! Pumped out? eh?" said Murray.

"If I am, there's plenty more like me," replied the Doctor enigmatically, "and some of them three times over! James, did these gentlemen leave you a drop of anything that you'd offer me?"

"Maybe ye'd like a glass of rum, Doctor?" said Mr. Canty with a wink at his other guests.

Dr. Hickey shuddered.

I had next morning precisely the kind of mouth that I had anticipated, and it being my duty to spend the better part of the day administering justice in Skebawn, I received from Mr. Flurry Knox and other of my brother magistrates precisely the class of condolences on my "Monday head" that I found least amusing. It was unavailing to point out the resemblance between hot potato cakes and molten lead, or to dilate on their equal power of solidifying; the collective wisdom of the Bench decided that I was suffering from contraband rum, and rejoiced over me accordingly.

During the next three weeks Murray and Bosanquet put in a time only to be equalled by that of the heroes in detective romances. They began by acting on the hint offered by Mr. Canty, and were rewarded by finding eight barrels of bacon and three casks of rum in the heart of Mr. Sullivan's turf rick, placed there, so Mr. Sullivan explained with much detail, by enemies, with the object of getting his license taken away. They stabbed potato gardens with crowbars to find the buried barrels, they explored the chimneys, they raided the cow-houses; and in every possible and impossible place they found some of the cargo of the late barque *John D. Williams,* and, as the sympathetic Mr. Canty said, "For as much as they found, they left five times as much afther them!"

It was a wet, lingering autumn, but towards the end of November the rain dried up, the weather stiffened, and a week of light frosts and blue skies was offered as a tardy apology. Philippa possesses, in common with many of her sex, an inappeasable passion for picnics, and her ingenuity for devising occasions for them is only equalled by her gift for enduring their rigors. I have seen her tackle a moist chicken pie with a splinter of slate and my stylograph pen. I have known her to take the tea-basket to an auction, and make tea in a four-wheeled inside car, regardless of the fact that it was coming under the hammer in ten minutes, and that the kettle took twenty minutes to boil. It will therefore be readily understood that the rare occasions when I was free to go out with a gun were not allowed to pass uncelebrated by the tea-basket.

"You'd much better shoot Corran Lake tomorrow," my wife said to me one brilliant afternoon. "We could send the punt over, and I could meet you on Holy Island with—"

The rest of the sentence was concerned with ways, means and the tea-basket, and need not be recorded.

I had taken the shooting of a long snipe bog that trailed from Corran Lake almost to the sea at Tralagough, and it was my custom to begin to shoot from the seaward end of it, and finally to work round the lake after duck.

Tomorrow proved a heavenly morning, touched with frost, gilt with sun. I started early, and the mists were still smoking up from the calm, all-reflecting lake, as the Quaker stepped out along the level road, smashing the thin ice on the puddles with his big feet. Behind the calves of my legs sat Maria, Philippa's brown Irish water-spaniel, assiduously licking the barrels of my gun, as was her custom when the ecstasy of going out shooting was hers. Maria had been given to Philippa as a wedding-present, and since then it had been my wife's ambition that she should conform to the Beth Gelert standard of being "a lamb at home, a lion in the chase." Maria did pretty well as a lion: she hunted all dogs unmistakably smaller than herself, and whenever it was reasonably possible to do so she devoured the spoils of the chase, notably jack snipe. It was as a lamb that she failed; objectionable as I have no doubt a lamb would be as a domestic pet, it at least would not snatch the cold beef from the luncheon-table, nor yet, if banished for its crimes, would it spend the night in scratching the paint off the hall door. Maria bit beggars (who valued their disgusting limbs at five shillings the square inch), she bullied the servants, she concealed ducks' claws and fishes' backbones behind the sofa cushions, and yet, when she laid her brown snout upon my knee, and rolled her blackguard amber eyes upon me, and smote me with her feathered paw, it was impossible to remember her iniquities against her. On shooting mornings Maria ceased to be a buccaneer, a glutton, and a hypocrite. From the moment when I put my gun together her breakfast stood untouched until it suffered the final degradation of being eaten by the cats, and now in the trap she was shivering with excitement, and agonizing in her soul lest she should even yet be left behind.

Slipper met me at the cross roads from which I had sent back the trap; Slipper, redder in the nose than anything I had ever seen off the stage, very husky as to the voice, and going rather tender on both feet. He informed me that I should have a grand day's shooting, the head-poacher of the locality having, in a most gentlemanlike manner, refrained from exercising his sporting rights the day before, on hearing that I was coming. I understood that this was to be considered as a mark of high personal esteem, and I set to work at the bog with suitable gratitude.

In spite of Mr. O'Driscoll's magnanimity, I had not a very good morning. The snipe was there, but in the perfect stillness of the weather it was impossible to get near them, and five times out of six they were up, flickering and dodging, before I was within shot. Maria became possessed of seven devils and broke away from heel the first time I let off my gun, ranging far and wide in search of the bird I had missed, and putting up every live thing for half a mile round, as she went splashing and steeple-chasing through the bog. Slipper expressed his opinion of her behavior in language more appallingly picturesque and resourceful than any I had heard, even in the Skebawn Courthouse; I admit that at the time I thought he spoke very suitably. Before she was recaptured every remaining snipe within earshot was lifted out of it by Slipper's steam-engine whistles and my own infuriated bellows; it was fortunate that the bog was spacious and that there was still a long tract of it ahead, where beyond these voices there was peace.

I worked my way on, jumping treacle-dark drains, floundering through the rustling yellow rushes, circumnavigating the bog-holes, and taking every possible and impossible chance of a shot; by the time I had reached Corran Lake I had got two-and-a-half brace, retrieved by Maria with a perfection that showed what her powers were when the sinuous adroitness of Slipper's woodbine stick was fresh in her mind. But with Maria it was always the unexpected that happened. My last snipe, a jack, fell in the lake, and Maria, bursting through the reeds with kangaroo bounds, and cleaving the water like a torpedo-boat, was a model of all the virtues of her kind. She picked up the bird with a snake-like dart of her head, clambered with it on to a tussock, and there, well out of reach of the arm of the law, before our indignant eyes crunched it twice and bolted it.

"Well," said Slipper complacently, some ten minutes afterwards, "divil such a bating ever I gave a dog since the day Prince kill owld Mrs. Knox's peacock! Prince was a lump of a brown tarrier I had one time, and faith I kicked the toes out o' me owld boots on him before I had the owld lady composed!"

However composing Slipper's methods may have been to Mrs. Knox, they had quite the contrary effect upon a family party of duck that had been lying in the reeds. With horrified outcries they broke into flight, and now were far away on the ethereal mirror of the lake, among strings of their fellows that were floating and quacking in preoccupied indifference to my presence.

A promenade along the lake-shore demonstrated the fact that without a boat there was no more shooting for me; I looked across to the island where, some time ago, I had seen Philippa and her punt arrive. The boat was tied to an overhanging tree, but my wife was nowhere to be seen. I was opening my mouth to give a hail, when I saw her emerge precipitately from among the trees and jump into the boat; Philippa had not in vain spent many summers on the Thames, she was under way in a twinkling, sculled a score of strokes at the rate of a finish, then stopped and stared at the peaceful island. I called to her, and in a minute or two the punt had crackled through the reeds, and shoved its blunt nose ashore at the spot where I was standing.

"Sinclair,'" said Philippa in awe-struck tones, "there's something on the island!"

"I hope there's something to eat there," said I.

"I tell you there *is* something there, alive," said my wife with her eyes as large as saucers; "it's making an awful sound like snoring."

"That's the fairies, ma'am," said Slipper with complete certainty; "sure I know them that seen fairies in that island as thick as the grass, and every one o' them with little caps on them."

Philippa's wide gaze wandered to Slipper's hideous pug face and back to me.

"It was not a human being, Sinclair!" she said combatively, though I had not uttered a word.

Maria had already, after the manner of dogs, leaped, dripping, into the boat: I prepared to follow her example.

"Major," said Slipper, in a tragic whisper, "there was a man was a night on that island one time, watching duck, and Thim People cot him, and dhragged him through Hell and through Death, and threw him in the tide—"

"Shove off the boat," I said too hungry for argument.

Slipper obeyed, throwing his knee over the gunwale as he did so, and tumbling into the bow; we could have done without him very comfortably, but his devotion was touching.

Holy Island was perhaps a hundred yards long, and about half as many broad; it was covered with trees and a dense growth of rhododendrons; somewhere in the jungle was a ruined fragment of a chapel, smothered in ivy and briars, and in a little glade in the heart of the island there was a holy well. We landed, and it was obviously a sore humiliation to Philippa that not a sound was to be heard in the spellbound silence of the island, save the cough of a heron on a tree-top.

"It *was* there," she said, with an unconvinced glance at the surrounding thickets.

"Sure, I'll give a thrawl through the island, ma'am," volunteered Slipper with unexpected gallantry, "an' if it's the divil himself is in it, I'll rattle him into the lake!"

He went swaggering on his search, shouting, "Hi, cock!" and

whacking the rhododendrons with his stick, and after an interval returned and assured us that the island was uninhabited. Being provided with refreshments he again withdrew, and Philippa and Maria and I fed variously and at great length, and washed the plates with water from the holy well. I was smoking a cigarette when we heard Slipper addressing the solitudes at the farther end of the island, and ending with one of his whiskey-throated crows of laughter.

He presently came lurching towards us through the bushes, and a glance sufficed to show even Philippa—who was as incompetent a judge of such matters as many of her sex—that he was undeniably screwed.

"Major Yeates!" he began, "and Mrs. Major Yeates, with respex to ye, I'm bastely dhrunk! Me head is light since the 'fluenzy, and the doctor told me I should carry a little bottle-een o' sperrits—"

"Look here," I said to Philippa, "I'll take him across, and bring the boat back to you."

"Sinclair," responded my wife with concentrated emotion, "I would rather die than stay on this island alone!"

Slipper was getting drunker every moment, but I managed to stow him on his back in the bows of the punt, in which position he at once began to uplift husky and wandering strains of melody. To this accompaniment we, as Tennyson says,

> Moved from the brink like some full-breasted swan,
> That, fluting a wild carol ere her death,
> Ruffles her pure cold plume, and takes the flood
> With swarthy web.

Slipper would certainly have been none the worse for taking the flood, and, as the burden of "Lannigan's Ball" strengthened and spread along the tranquil lake, and the duck once more fled in justifiable consternation, I felt much inclined to make him do so.

We made for the end of the lake that was nearest Shreelane, and, as we rounded the point of the island, another boat presented itself to our view. It contained my late entertainer, Mrs. Canty, seated bulkily in the stern, while a small boy bowed himself between the two heavy oars.

"It's a lovely evening, Major Yeates," she called out, "I'm just going to the island to get some water from the holy well for me daughter that has an impression on her chest. Indeed, I thought 'twas yourself was singing a song for Mrs. Yeates when I heard you coming, but sure Slipper is a great warrant himself for singing."

"May the divil crack the two legs undher ye!" bawled Slipper in acknowledgement of the compliment.

Mrs. Canty laughed genially, and her boat lumbered away.

I shoved Slipper ashore at the nearest point. Philippa and I paddled to the end of the lake, and abandoning the duck as a bad business, walked home.

A few days afterwards it happened that it was incumbent upon me to attend the funeral of the Roman Catholic Bishop of the diocese. It was what is called in France *um bel enterrement,* with inky flocks of tall-hatted priests, and countless yards of white scarves, and a repast of monumental solidity at the Bishop's residence. The actual interment was to take place in Cork, and we moved in long and imposing procession to the railway station, where a special train awaited the cortège. My friend Mr. James Canty was among the mourners: an important and active personage, exchanging condolences with the priests, giving directions to porters, and blowing his nose with a trumpeting mournfulness that penetrated all the other noises of the platform. He was condescending enough to notice my presence, and found time to tell me that he had given Mr. Murray "a sure word" with regard to some of *"the wreckage"*—this with deep significance, and a wink of an inflamed and tearful eye. I saw him depart in a first-class carriage, and the odor of sanctity; seeing that he was accompanied by seven priests, and that both windows were shut, the latter must have been considerable.

Afterwards, in the town, I met Murray, looking more pleased with himself than I had seen him since he had taken up the unprofitable task of smuggler-hunting.

"Come along and have some lunch," he said, "I've got a real good thing on this time! That chap Canty came to me late last night, and told me he knew for a fact that the island on Corran Lake was just stiff with barrels of bacon and rum, and that I'd better send every man I could spare today to get them into the town. I sent the men out at eight o'clock this morning; I think I've gone one better than Bosanquet this time!"

I began to realize that Philippa was going to score heavily on the subject of the fairies that she had heard snoring on the island, and I imparted to Murray the leading features of our picnic there.

"Oh, Slipper's been up to his chin in that rum from the first," said Murray. "I'd like to know who his sleeping partner was!"

It was beginning to get dark before the loaded carts of the salvage party came lumbering past Murray's windows and into the yard of the police-barrack. We followed them, and in so doing picked up Flurry Knox, who was sauntering in the same direction. It was a good haul, five big casks of rum, and at least a dozen smaller barrels of bacon and butter, and Murray and his Chief Constable smiled seraphically on one another as the spoil was unloaded and stowed in a shed.

"Wouldn't it be as well to see how the butter is keeping?" remarked Flurry, who had been looking on silently, with, as I had noticed, a still and amusing eye. "The rim of that small keg there looks as if it had been shifted lately."

The sergeant looked hard at Flurry; he knew as well as most people that a hint from Mr. Knox was usually worth taking. He turned to Murray.

"Will I open it, Sir?"

"Oh! open it if Mr. Knox wishes," said Murray, who was not famous for appreciating other people's suggestions.

The keg was opened.

"Funny butter," said Flurry.

The sergeant said nothing. The keg was full of black bog-mould. Another was opened, and another, all with the same result.

"Damnation!" said Murray, suddenly losing his temper. "What's the use of going on with those? Try one of the rum casks?"

A few moments passed in total silence while a tap and a spigot were sent for and applied to the barrel. The sergeant drew off a mugful and put his nose to it with the deliberation of a connoisseur.

"Water, sir," he pronounced, "dirty water, with a small indication of sperrits."

A junior constable tittered explosively, met the light blue glare of Murray's eye, and withered away.

"Perhaps it's holy water!" said I, with a wavering voice.

Murray's glance pinned me like an assegaii, and I also faded into the background.

"Well," said Flurry in dulcet tones, "if you want to know where the stuff is that was in those barrels, I can tell you, for I was told it myself half-an-hour ago. It's gone to Cork with the Bishop by special train!"

Mr. Canty was undoubtedly a man of resource. Mrs. Canty had mistakenly credited me with an intelligence equal to her own, and on receiving from Slipper a highly colorful account of how audibly Mr. Canty had slept off his potations, had regarded the secret of Holy Island as having been given away. That night and the two succeeding ones were spent in the transfer of the rum to bottles, and the bottles and the butter to fish boxes; these were, by means of a slight lubrication of the railway underlings loaded into a truck as "Fresh Fish, Urgent," and attached to the Bishop's funeral train, while the police, decoyed far from the scene of action, were breaking their backs over barrels of bog-water. "I suppose," continued Flurry pleasantly, "you don't know the pub that Canty's brother has in Cork. Well, I do. I'm going to buy some rum there next week, cheap."

"I shall proceed against Canty!" said Murray, with fateful calm.

"You won't proceed far," said Flurry; "you'll not get as much evidence out of the whole country as'd hang a cat."

"Who was your informant?" demanded Murray.

Flurry laughed. "Well, by the time the train was in Cork, yourself and the Major were the only two men in the town that weren't talking about it."

The Bewitched Fiddle
Seamus MacManus

FAIX, it's a long long wheen of years since it happened now. It was ould Jimmy Higgerty, that was uncle to Mickey acrass there, reharsed the passage to me. An' it was ould Jimmy himself, more betoken, that was the cause of the whole affair—for Jimmy, ye know, was what we call a canny man, very knowin' intirely, an' up to all sorts of saicrets that you nor me nor one belonging to us, thanks be to Providence, knows nothin' at all, at all about. Jimmy was right-han' man with the fairies; an' if y'd believe all the stories ye hear goin' he come through some quare things, too, in his day—used to be out, they say, as reg'lar as the sunset, an' away ridin' aist an' waist with the good people, an' gettin' insight into their ways of workin'; an' sure it's meself that rec'le'ts if there was only a bit of a year-oul' calve sick from one end of the barony to the other, it was nothin' but post haste for Jimmy Higgerty to cure it—an', sure enough, when Jimmy put the charm on it, it either lived or died afther; there was no middle coorse.

Well, howsomiver, in Jimmy's day there was in Doorin a one Solomon Casshidy; an' the same Solomon in his young days was a thrifle wild—the fact is (to kill the hare at a blow), Solomon was the completest rascal ivir run on two feet, an' was a parable for the counthry. Christenin', weddin', wake, funeral, patthern, fair, or market nivir wint off complete without Solomon Casshidy; dance, raffle, or spree of any sort, shape, or patthern nivir missed Solomon Casshidy, who, by the way, was the very life an' sowl of the gatherin's; an' people would as soon think of doin' without the fiddler at one of these merry-makin's as without Solomon Casshidy. An' that just put me in mind that Solomon was the dandy hand at the fiddle; the bate of him wasn't to be got between cock-crow an' candlelight the longest day in June. He would charm the heart of a whin-bush; arrah, good luck to your wit, man, he'd actually make the fiddle spake! They say it was as good as a sarcus to hear how he'd handle it.

But poor Solomon, good luck to him, soon came to the end of his tether, an', after takin' all the fun he could out of the worl', he, as himself said, turned over a new laif an' begun to look at the other side

of the picther. An' I'm thinkin' whatsomiver he seen on the other side
of it must have been deuced onpleasant, for the rollickin', singin',
laughin', fiddlin', reckless, ne'er-do-well Solomon pulled a face on
him the length of a tailyer's lapboord, an' if any of his ould comrades
attimpted to make him convarsible on the fun that was goin' in any
quarther of the counthry, Solomon would dhrop his jaws, an' fetch a
groan would frighten a corp'; an' "My Fren", he would say, "this is all
vanity, vanity! Life is hollow, an' these frivolities are only snares
spread in our paths by the divil."

Anyhow, Solomon was an althered man, an' where he would go
formerly to honor the Sabbath by a rousin' game of *caman* with the
good boys, he was now seen makin' his way to the meetin'-house with
a Bible anondher his arm the size of a salt-box, an' as many hime-
books as would set up a hawker in a daicent way of thradin', an' he
obsarvin' naither to the right nor to the left, but away a thousand miles
ahead of him, as if he was always thryin' to make out the way to
heaven somewhere in the skies foreninst him; an' where he would of
another time be makin' his way across the counthry, maybe to the
shouldher of Srual mountain for a spree, with the fiddle anondher his
coat, ye might now meet him in the dusk of the evenin', still with the
fiddle ondher the coat, but on a far betther errand—goin' to some
prayer-meetin' at Inver, or Killymard, or Ballywell, or the divil only
knows where; he wouldn't go within an ass's roar of a raffle-house;
an' if you tould him there was to be a dance or any other wee divarshin
in sich and sich a place he'd strive to put the breadth of a townlan'
betwixt him an' it, for he said the divil was chained to the back-stone
of any house that there was a hornpipe played in.

Well, one evenin', it was in October, an' jist about night-fallin',
Solomon was makin' his way for Billy Knox's of the head of the
Glibe, where a great and very pious man, one Bartholomew Binjamin
Rankin, was to hold a prayer-meetin' for the benefit of all the well-
disposed sinners in that stretch of counthry; an' throth, it seems to me
that, onless the Glibe's changed mortially within the last jinnyration,
there must have been a daicent quantity of sinners in them same parts.
But, as I was sayin', Solomon was this evenin' on the good arrand,
with his fiddle peepin' out from ondher his coat—for ye see,
Solomon's ould practice whin he was a sinner come in handy now that

he was a saint, an' no prayer-meetin' could be held without Solomon's fiddle to steady the voices, when they joined to sing the himes. She was a splendid piece of a fiddle, an' Solomon, when he turned over the new laif, was goin' out to brak her neck across the nixt ditch, when he remimbered how she might come in handy this way, so he said to himself (as he tould afther), that "he'd make the occasion of his sins a steppin'-stone to new vartues, an' cause her that was hairtofore jiggin' him down to the place below, now fiddle him into heaven."

He thought to himself this evenin' that he'd jist light the pipe to keep him company as he jogged on, so where do ye think he'd dhrop into, on purpose to light it, but ould Jimmy Higgerty's, the fairyman's, that I rehearsed to yet about before. On layin' "Pagganinny," as he called the fiddle, down on a stool, whilst he was puttin' a screed of coal to the pipe, Jimmy Higgerty lifted her, an' dhrawin' the bow acrass her, he took a bar of a lively tune out of her, when Solomon jumped up as if he was sthruck.

"Higgerty, me good man," he says, "you have shocked me. Thim vain airs," siz he, "has been long unknown to that fiddle, an' I trusted that she would nivir more be an insthrument that the divil would gamble for sowls on. Paice, paice, and dhraw not the bow in idle vanity again!'"

"Arrah, good morra to ye," siz Jimmy, that way back to him, "but it's delicate yer narves must have got intirely, lately. Throth, Misther Casshidy, I seen the time this wouldn't frighted ye one bit'"; an' all at oncet he sthruck up, "Go to the divil an' shake yerself," while poor Solomon stood thrimblin' in the middle of the flure like a man with the aguey. While Jimmy finished up with a flourish that would have delighted Solomon the days he was a himself (for, be the same token, Solomon was no miss at handlin' the bow naither), he cut some quare figures with his left han' three times over the fiddle, an' handin' it to Solomon, he says, "May ye nivir have more raison to be frightened than by a jig from the same fiddle—*that's all I say!*"

Poor Solomon didn't know the hidden mainin' of them words, or it would have made him look crooked; nor he didn't know naither that Jimmy had put *pisherogues* on the fiddle; but all the same he took it from him with a glum look enough, and afther praichin' an edifyin' sarmon on frivolities, an' death an' jedgment, to Jimmy Higgerty, he betook him on the road again.

There was a wonderful congregation of the sinners an' saints of the Glibe—but the sinners had the best of it anyhow, in regards to numbers—in Bill Knox's that nigh. An' Bartholomew Binjamin Rankin was there, an' it was as good as a sarmin in itself just to get one glance at his face. There was as much holiness an' piety in it, ye'd a'most think, as would save the sowls of a whole barony. Solomon, who now got all sorts an' sizes of respect, as bein' a reformed sinner, an' was looked up to with ten times as much honor and rivirence as was paid to them that was saints all their life, got a salt, as was usual, beside the praicher. An' it's himself that was proud, an' he'd look down on the common crowd below with a most pityin' look on his face. An' the well-disposed ones in the congregation would look up at Solomon an' then give a groan that ye might hear at Srual; an' Solomon would look down on the sinners an' give another groan that ye might hear him at Barnesmore; an' then both Solomon an' the sinners would look up at the rafthers, an' give a groan that ye might hear at Muckish. Afther some time, when they had got faistin' their sowls fairly well on Solomon, a hime was called out, a very solemn one. "An," says the praicher, lookin' at Solomon, "our saintly brother here, of whom aich and ivery heart in this gatherin' feels proud, an' whose pious ways are the glorification, admiration, and' edifycation of every true Christian since he gave up his ungodly life, an' turned onto the path of righteousness—brother Solomon will give us the keynote, an' lend us the aid of his unmusical box, throughout."

Brother Solomon, be me socks, dhrew a face on him the length of his own fiddle, as if he was thinkin' of his own unworthiness, poor man, an' says:

"If affords me a pious pleasure to dhraw my bow ondher the circumstances—that bow which so often snared me into the divil's sarvice; but I thank God with my heart that I have long since departed from my wicked, wicked, unspaikably vile an' sinful ways; an' this han' has long since forgotten them vain and ungodly airs that at one time occupied every spare moment of my then onChristian life—long since, I say, have I buried deep in obliveen every remimbrance of thim wicked tunes, an' the cunnin' of my han' is now only used for a far loftier an' betther purpose. Bretherin, I shall begin."

And Solomon dhraws the bow across the fidle, an' of all the himes tunes which was prented, what do y think does he sthrike up? "Go to the divil an' shake yerself!" Och, it's as thrue as I'm telling it to ye. But, *ochón,* if there wasn't consternation in that house, I'm a gintleman! Solomon himself stopped suddent, for all the world lookin' like a stuck pig; an' he looked at the praicher, an' the praicher looked at him. and the congregation looked at both of them, and then Solomon prayed from his heart as he nivir prayed afore, that the Lord in His marcy might make the flure open and swallow him. The flure, though, as I suppose ye have guessed, did not open, but Bartholomew Binjamin's mouth did, an' he sayed, siz he:

"Bretherin! bretherin! this is a sad fallin' away! Alas! alas! Who should have thought that Brother Solomon, the deformed sinner, would have returned to his ould godless coorses! the rulin' passion, my dear bretherin, is so sthrong in him—waxin' sthrong with new strength—that he has onvoluntarily bethrayed the divil that has again got hould on him. Bretherin, let us pray for him!"

An' in a jiffy the thunderstruck congregation were on their knees prayin' like Trojans for the delivery of poor Solomon from the divil. Solomon, of course, for appairance' sake, had to take to his knees, too, but between you an' me, it's meself's afeard that all the prayers he said would not fetch him very far on the way to the first milestone that leads to heaven. I'll wager whoivir heerd him, that his prayers were sweet ones, that the divil might saize ould Jimmy Higgerty an' carry him off body an' bones, an' give him a toastin' on a special griddle down below. When they thought they had prayed long enough, an' that the divil was gone out of Solomon, they got up to their feet again, and they turned up the whites of their eyes till Bartholomew Binjamin announced that they would oncest more put Brother Solomon's faith to the test, to see if he had profited by the few minutes' sperritial recreation that they had indulged in. Solomon lifted the bow, an' afore he started he turned up the whites of his eyes in the usual fashion, as if he was lookin' for guidance, but in his heart he was only callin' down another black curse on Jimmy Higgerty.

"Bretherin!" siz he, as solemn as a judge—"Bretherin! the temper' (by which he meant the divil of coorse) "'possessed the fiddle, and not my humble self; in witness whereof just attind to the solemn an' addyfyin' air I will now produce for ye." An' down comes the bow on the fiddle, an' up starts that beautiful jig tune, "The Siege of Carrick"!

Och, tarnation to me waistcoat, but there was sich a scene in two minnits as would charm a dancin' masther! When Solomon played the first bar of it, he could as soon comb his head with his toes as he could stop it. But that wasn't the best of it. Bartholomew Binjamin, instead of goin' into a cowld dead faint, as one would expect, begun to shuffle his feet in a suspicious way, an' afore ye'd say "thrapsticks" he was weltin' the flure like the broth of a boy, tearin' away at the jig like the ould Nick! An' in the squintin' of yer eye there wasn't a sowl anondher the roof, man, woman, or child, saint or sinner, that wasn't whackin' away at it like the forties, iviry man of them leatherin' the flure like a thrasher, jumpin' up till their heads would a'most sthrike the rafters, an' yellin like red Injins, whilst me brave Solomon played like a black, put new life into the fiddle at ivery squeak, an' gave the jiggers whativer wee encouragement that he could spare time from the fiddle for:

"Come, boys, yez haven't fair play to foot it properly here. Yez is the finest set at a jig that I have faisted me eyes on since I give up me ungodly ways, an' it would be a pity for not to give yez ivery privilege —it's a fine clear moonlight, an' we'll go outside where we'll have room an' fair play at it. Come along, me mirry, mirry lads!" An' Solomon fiddled away out of the dure, an' the whole congregation leapt an' flung an' jigged it out in all possible an' onpossible shapes afther him. Och, they say it was a sight for sore eyes to see the capers that the party cut; ivery man jack of them tryin' to see who could be crazier than his naybor; an' out they got that way on the road, like a lunatic asylum turned loose for a holiday; an' Solomon headed down the road in the direction of Donegal, while the whole contryside turned out when they heard the yellin' an' fiddlin' an' prancin', an' seein' Solomon headin' them with the fiddle, an' Bartholomew Binjamin fillin' the front rank in company with his two feet, an' he jiggin' it away at the rate of a christenin'! The people were first inclined to laugh, but be the powdhers that nixt thing they done was join in themselves, an' foot it way afther the fiddle ninety-nine times crazier than the congregation. An' hot foot they kept it goin', up hill an' down dale, over height an' hollow, with fresh batches joinin' in at ivery lane

an' turn, an' Solomon, the boy, layin' into the fiddle at a rate as if he
was gettin' a salary for it; an', be the boots, by the time they raiched
the foot of the road, you niver seem in all your born days a harvest fair
or a Repale meetin' as big as it was!

Here Solomon turned to the left, with the purcession still jiggin' it
afther him, an' he nixt got onto the lane that leads up to the Killymard
ould graveyard, an' over the stile, in among the graves with the mirry
company brakin' their necks over, afther him; an' when they got in
here, Solomon made thracks for a nate dandy bit of a tombstone in the
center of the yard, an' upon it he h'isted himself, with Bartholomew
Binjamin up beside him, whilst the remainder of the party reshumed
their attitudes all roun' about, an' they fightin' like wild cats to see
who would get pursession of the tombstones, for they say they wer as
good as barn-doors for dancin' on. An' throgs, there might be purty
good dancers there, but divil resave the one of them that Solomon and
Bartholomew Binjamin couldn't take the shine out of it. They had a
bran' new tombstone, the pick an' choice of all in the yard, an' if they
didn't do it in royal style, an' cut a copy to the crowd, call me a
cuckoo!

But what would ye have of it, but the nixt man lands on the scene
was Sandy Montgomery, the Recthor. He was passin' the road, an'
seein' the fun in the graveyard, he come up in a t'undherin' passion to
horsewhip iviry mother's sowl of them. But, sweet good luck to ye, if
he didn't jump up on the fiddler's tombstone, an' catchin'
Bartholomew Binjamin by the han', foot it away, likewise.

An' it would have gone on to daylight in the mornin', if ould
Jimmy Higgerty, the rascal, who followed the fun the whole way from
the Glibe, for the purpose of tastifyin' to it—if he hadn't come behin'
Solomon an' tould him to kick up his right heel, dhraw his left thumb
three times over the sthrings of the fiddle, an' look over his left
shouldher at the moon, an' then see what music he'd take out of it. No
sooner sayed nor done; an' all at once the tune changed to a hime tune,
all mournful, an' iviry heel in the graveyard was paralyzed. Ivery sowl
of them looked at one another like they wor wakenin' out of a dhraim.

Solomon himself dhrew up, an' he gave a bewildhered look all
roun' him, an' then looked at Sandy Montgomery, who was standin'
forenenst him on the stone, an' he as pale as a sheet. Ivery man of the

three on the thombstone gave themselves up as lost men, ruinated intirely, out an' out, afther making' such spectacles of themselves for the counthry. The Recthor lost conthrol of himself completely, an' puttin' his fist anondher Solomon's nose, he says:

"Ye common scoundhril, ye; ye've made me disgrace my cloth, ye cut-throat villain—"

But afore he could get another word, Solomon, who had some of the spunk of his early days in him still, and was a thrifle hasty, besides that his dandher was riz in regards to the purty pickle he was in— Solomon ups with the fiddle, an' dhrawin' it roun' his head with a swing, he takes the Recthor across the noddfle an' knocked him a'most into kingdom come, away off the tombstone. But, my hearty, in swingin' the fiddle, doesn't he catch Bartholomew Binjamin, who was standin' behind him, a nate little bit of a knock on the skull. So, now turnin' round to apologize to him, Bartholomew Binjamin ups with his fist an' plants it undher Solomon's nose, too, for he was just commencin' a norration.

"Ye mane, onprincipled, ungodly bla'guard!"

But Solomon couldn't stand this neither. He says to himself he might as well be hung for a sheep as a lamb, and that when he knocked down a Recthor, he might with an asier conscience knock down a praicher. So he took the praicher a wallop with the fiddle that left him sprawlin' in the Recthor's lap with his heels uppermost, and Solomon leapt from the tombstone, an' off through the crowd for the bare life, wallopin' them right an' left. They all slunk home afther a while with their tails between their legs, but poor Solomon was the worst of all. He made "Pagganinny" into smithereens—what remained of her. An' he didn't lift his head for twelve months afther.

Little Fairly
Samuel Lover

THE WORDS GREAT AND LITTLE are sometimes contradictory terms to
their own meaning. This is stating the case rather confusedly, but as I
am an Irishman, and writing an Irish story, it is the more in character. I
might do perhaps, like a very clever and agreeable friend of mine,
who, when he deals in some extravagance which you don't quite
understand, says, "Well, you know what I mean," But I will not take
that for granted, so what I mean is that—that your great man, (as far as
size is concerned), is often a nobody; and your little man, is often a
great man. Nature, as far as the human race is concerned, is at variance
with Art, which generally couples greatness with size. The pyramids,
the temple of Jupiter Olympius, St. Peter's, and St. Paul's, are vast in
their dimensions, and the heroes of Painting and Sculpture are always
on a grand scale. In Language, the *diminutive* is indicative of
endearment—in Nature, it appears to me, it is the type of distinction.
Alexander, Caesar, Napoleon, Wellington, etc. etc. (for I have not
room to detail) are instances. But do we not hear every day that "such-
a-body is a big booby," while "*a clever little fellow*" has almost passed
into a proverb. The poets have been more true to nature than painters,
in this particular, and in her own divine art, her happiest votaries have
been living evidences of her predilection to "packing her choicest
goods in small parcels." Pope was "a crooked little thing that asked
questions," and in your own days, our own "little Moore" is a glorious
testimony to the fact. The works of fiction abound with instances, that
the author does not consider it necessary his hero shall be an eligible
candidate for the "grenadier corps"; the earlier works of fiction in
particular: Fairy tales, universally, dedicate some *giant* to destruction
at the hands of some "clever little fellow." "Tom Thumb," "Jack and
the Bean Stalk," and fifty other such for instance, and I am now going
to add another to the list, a brilliant example, I trust, of the unfailing
rule, that your *little* man is always a *great* man.

If any gentleman six foot two inches high gets angry at reading this,
I beg him to remember that I am a little man myself, and if he be a
person of sense (which is supposing a great deal), he will pardon, from

57

his own feeling of indignation of this *exposé* of Patagonian inferiority, the consequent triumph, on my part, of Lilliputian distinction. If, however, his inches get the better of him, and he should call me out, I bcg of him to remember, again, that I have the advantage of him there too, in being a little man. There is a proverb also, that "*little* said is soon mended," and with all my preaching, I fear I have been forgetting the wholesome adage. So I shall conclude this little introduction, which I only thought a becoming flourish of trumpets for introducing my hero, by placing *Little Fairly* before my readers, and I hope they will not think, in the words of another adage, that I have given them *great* cry and *little* wool.

You see owld Fairly was a mighty dacent man that lived, as the story goes, out over the back o' the hills beyant there, and was a thrivin' man ever afther he married little Shane Ruadh's[1] daughther, and she was little, like her father before her, a dawnshee craythur, but mighty cute, and industhered a power, always, and a fine wife she was to a sthrivin' man, up early and down late, and shure if she was doin' nothin' else, the bit iv a stocking was never out iv her hand, and the knittin' needles goin' like mad. Well, sure they thruv like a flag or a bulrush, and the snuggest cabin in the counthry side was owld Fairly's. And, in due coorse she brought him a son, throth she lost no time about it either, for she was never given to loitherin', and he was the picthur o' the mother, the little attomy that he was, as slim as a ferret and as red as a fox, but a hardy craythur. Well, owld Fairly didn't like the thoughts of havin' sitch a bit iv a brat for a son, and besides he thought he got on so well and prospered in the world with one wife, that, by gor, he determined to improve his luck and get another. So, with that, he ups and goes to one Doody, who had a big daughter—a whopper, by my sowl! throth she was the full of a door, and was called by the neighbors *garran more*,[2] for in throth she was a garran, the dirty dhrop was in her, a nasty stag that never done a good turn for any one but herself; the long-sided jack, that she was, but her father had a power o' money, and above a hundher head o' cattle, and divil a chick

1. *Red John.*

2. *Big Horse.*

nor child he had but herself, so that she was a great catch for whoever could get her, as far as the fortin' wint; but throth, the boys did not like the looks iv her, and let herself and her fortin' alone. Well, as I was sayin', owld Fairly ups and he goes to Doody and puts his *comether* an the girl, and faix she was glad to be ax'd, and so matthers was soon settled, and the ind of it was they wor married.

Now maybe it's axin' you'd be how he could marry two wives at wanst; but I towld you before, it was long ago, in the good owld ancient times, whin a man could have plinty of every thing. So, home he brought the dirty garran, and sorra long was she in the place whin she began to breed, (arrah, lave off and don't be laughin' now; I don't mane that at all,) whin she began to breed *ructions* in the fam'ly, and to kick up *antagions* from mornin' till night, and *put betune* owld Fairly and his first wife. Well, she had a son of her own soon, and he was a big boss iv a divil, like his mother—a great fat lob that had no life in him at all; and while the little daunshee craythur would laugh in your face and play wid you if you cherrup'd to him, or would amuse himself, the craythur, crawlin' about the flure and playin' wid the sthraws, and atein' the gravel, the jewel,—the other bosthoon was roarin' from mornin' till night, barrin' he was crammed wid stirabout and dhrownded a'most wid milk. Well, up they grew, and the big chap turned out a *gommoch*, and the little chap was as knowin' as a jailor; and though the big mother was always puttin' up her lob to malthrate and abuse little Fairly, the dickins a one but the little chap used to sarcumvint him, and gev him no pace, but led him the life iv a dog wid the cunnin' thricks he played on him. Now, while all the neighbors a'most loved the ground that little Fairly throd on, they cudn't abide the garran more's foal, good, bad, or indifferent, and many's the sly *malavoguein'* he got behind a hedge, from one or another, when his mother or father wasn't to purtect him, for owld Fairly was as great a fool about him as the mother, and would give him his eyes, a'most to play marvels, while he didn't care three *thraneens* for the darlint little chap. And 'twas the one thing as long as he lived; and at last he fell sick, and sure many thought it was a judgment an him for his unnath'ral doin's to his own flesh and blood, and the sayin' through the parish was, from one and all, "There's owld Fairly is obleeged *to take to his bed with the weight of his sins.*" And sure enough off o' that same bed he never riz, but grew weaker and weaker every day, and sint for the priest to make his sowl, the wicked owld sinner, God forgive me for sayin' the word, and sure the priest done whatever he could for him; but after the priest wint away he called his two wives beside his bed, and the two sons, and says he, "I'm goin' to lave yiz now," says he, "and sorry I am," says he, "for I'd rather stay in owld Ireland than go anywhere else," says he, "for a raison I have—heigh! heigh! heigh!—Oh, murther, this cough is smotherin' me, so it is. Oh, wurra! wurra! but it's sick and sore I am. Well, come here yiz both," says he to the women, "you wor good wives both o' ye; I have nothin' to say agin it—(Molly, don't forget the whate is to be winny'd the first fine day)—and ready you wor to make and to mind—(Judy, there's a hole in the foot of my left stockin'), and—"

"Don't be thinkin' o' your footin' here," says little Judy, the knowledgable craythur, as she was, "but endayvour to make your footin' in heaven" says she, "mavourneen."

"Don't put in your prate 'till you re ax'd," says the owld savage, no ways obleeged that his trusty little owld woman was wantin' to give him a helpin' hand tow'rds puttin' his poor sinful sowl in the say o' glory.

"Lord look down on you!" says she.

"Tuck the blanket round my feet," says he, "for I'm gettin' very cowld."

So the big owld hag of a wife tucked the blankets round him.

"Ah, you were always a comfort to me," says owld Fairly.

"Well, remember my son for that same," says she, "for it's time I think you'd be dividin' what you have bechuxt uz," says she.

"Well, I suppose I must do it at last," says the owld chap, "though, hegh! hegh! hegh! Oh this thievin' cough—though it's hard to be obleeged to lave one's hard airnins and comforts this-a-way," says he, the unfort'nate owld thief, thinkin' o' this world instead of his own poor sinful sowl.

"Come here, big Fairly," says he, "my own bully boy, that's not a starved poor ferret, but worth while lookin' at. I lave you this house," says he.

"Ha!" says the big owld sthrap, makin' a face over the bed at the poor little woman that was cryin', the craythur, although the owld villain was usin' her so bad.

"And I lave you all my farms," says he.

"Ha!" says the big owld sthreel again.

"And my farmin' *ingraydients,*" says he.

"Ha!" says she again, takin' a pinch o' snuff.

"And *all* my cattle," says he.

"Did you hear that, ma'am?" says the garran more, stickin' her arms akimbo, and lookin' as if she was goin' to bate the woman.

"All my cattle," says the owld fellow, "every head," says he, "barrin' one, and that one is for that poor scaldcrow there," says he, "little Fairly."

"And is it only one you lave my poor boy?" says the poor little woman.

"If you say much," says the owld dyin' vagabond, "the divil resave the taste of any thing I'll lave him or you," says he.

"Don't say divil, darlin'".

"Howld your prate, I tell you, and listen to me. I say, you little Fairly."

"Well, daddy," says the little chap.

"Go over to that corner cupboard," says he, "and in the top shelf," says he, "in the bottom of a crack'd taypot, you'll find a piece of an owld rag, and bring it here to me."

With that little Fairly went to do as he was bid, but he could not reach up so high as the corner cupboard, and he run into the next room for a stool to stand upon to come at the crack'd taypot, and he got the owld piece iv a rag and brought it to his father.

"Open it," says the father.

"I have it open now," says little Fairly.

"What's in it?" says the owld boy.

"Six shillin's in silver, and three farthin's," says little Fairly.

"That was your mother's fortune," says the father, "and I'm goin' to behave like the hoighth of a gentleman, as I am," says he; "I'll give you your mother's fortune," says he, "and I hope you won't squandher it," says he, "the way that every blackguard now thinks he has a right to squandher any decent man's money he is the heir to," says he, "but be careful of it," says he, "as I was, for I never touched a rap iv it, but let it lie gotherin' in that taypot, ever since the day I got it from Shane

Ruadh, the day we sthruck the bargain about Judy, over beyant at the 'Cat and Bagpipes,' comin' from the fair; and I lave you that *six* shillings and *five* stone o'mouldy oats that's no use to me, and *four* broken plates, and that *three*-legged stool you stood upon to get at the cupboard, you poor *nharrough* that you are, and the *two* spoons without handles, and the *one* cow that's gone back of her milk."

"What use is the cow, daddy," says little Fairly, "widout land to feed her an?"

"Maybe it's land you want, you pinkeen," says the big brother.

"Right, my bully boy," says the mother, "stand up for your own."

"Well, well," says the owld chap, "I tell you what, big Fairly," says he, "you may as well do a dacent turn for the little chap, and give him grass for this cow. I lave you all the land," says he, "but you'll never miss grass for one cow," says he, "but you'll have the satisfaction of bein' bountiful to your little brother, bad cess to him, for a starved hound as he is."

But, to make a long story short, the ould chap soon had the puff out iv him; and whin the wake was over, and that they put him out to grass —laid him asleep, snug, with a *daisy quilt over him*—throth that minit the poor little woman and her *little offsprig* was turned out body and bones, and forced to seek shelter any way they could.

Well, little Fairly was a cute chap, and so he made a little snug place out of the back iv a ditch, and wid moss and rishes and laves and brambles, made his ould mother snug enough, antil he got a little mud cabin built for her, and the cow gev them milk, and the craythurs got on purty well, antil the big dirty vagabone of a brother began to grudge the cow the bit o' grass, and he ups and says he to little Fairly one day, "What's the raison," saye he, "your cow does be threspassin' an my fields?" says he.

"Sure and wasn't it the last dyin' words o' my father to you," says little Fairly, "that you would let me have grass for my cow?"

"I don't remember it," says big Fairly—the dirty naygur, who was put up to it all, by the garran more, his mother.

"Yiv a short memory," says little Fairly.

"Yis, but I've a long stick," says the big chap, shakin' it at him at the same time, "and I'd rekimmind you to keep a civil tongue in your head," says he.

"You're mighty ready to bate your little brother, but would you fight your match?" says little Fairly.

"Match or no match," says big Fairly, "I'll brake your bones if you give me more o' your prate," says he; "and I tell you again, don't let your cow be thresspassin' an my land, or I warn you that you'll be sorry," and off he wint.

Well, little Fairly kept never mindin' him, and brought his cow to graze every day on big Fairly's land; and the big fellow used to come and *hish* her off the land, but the cow was as little and cute as her mother—she was a Kerry cow, and there's a power o'cuteness comes out o' Kerry. Well, as I was saying, the cow used to go off as *quite* as a lamb; but the minit the big bosthoon used to turn his back, *whoo!* my jewel, she used to leap the ditch as clever as a hunther, and back wid her again to graze, and faix good use she made of her time, for she got brave and hearty, and geve a power o' milk, though she was goin' back of it shortly before, but there was a blessin' over Fairly, and all belongin' to him, and all that he put his hand to thruv with him. Well, now I must tell you what big Fairly done—and the dirty turn it was; but the dirt was in him ever and always, and kind mother it was for him. Well, what did he do but he dug big pits all through the field where little Fairly's cow used to graze, and he covers them up with branches o' trees and sods, makin' it look fair and even, and all as one as the rest o' the field, and with that he goes to little Fairly, and, says he, "I tould you before," says he, "not to be sendin' your little blackguard cow to thresspass on my fields," says he, "and mind I tell you now, that it won't be good for her health to let her go there again, for I tell you she'll come to harm, and it's dead she'll be before long."

"Well, she may as well die one way as another," says little Fairly, "for sure if she doesn't get grass she must die, and I tell you again, divil an off your land I'll take my cow."

"Can't you let your dirty cow graze along the road side?" says big Fairly.

"Why then do you think," says little Fairly, answering him mighty smart, "do you think I have so little respect for my father's cow as to turn her out a beggar an the road to get her dinner off the common highway? Throth I'll do no sitch thing."

"Well, you'll soon see the end iv it," says big Fairly, and off he wint in great delight, thinkin' how poor little Fairly's cow would be killed. And now wasn't he the dirty threacherous, black-hearted villain, to take advantage of a poor cow, and lay a thrap for the dumb baste?— but whin the dirty dhrop is in it must come out. Well, poor Fairly sent his cow to graze next mornin', but the poor little darlin' craythur fell into one o' the pits and was kilt; and when little Fairly kem for her in the evenin' there she was cowld and stiff, and all he had to do now was to sing *drimmin dhu dheelish* over her, and dhrag her home as well as he could, wid the help of some neighbors that pitied the craythur, and cursed the big bosthoon that done such a threacherous turn.

Well, little Fairly was the fellow to put the best face upon every thing; and so, instead of givin' in to fret, and makin' lamentations that would do him no good, by dad, he began to think how he could make the best of what happened, and the little craythur sharpened a knife immediantly, and began to shkin the cow, "and any how," says he, "the cow is good mate, and my ould mother and me'ill have beef for the winther."

"Thrue for you, little Fairly," said one of the neighbors was helpin' him, "and besides, the hide'ill be good to make soals for your brogues for many a long day."

"Oh, I'll do betther wid the hide nor that," says little Fairly.

"Why what better can you do nor that wid it?" says the neighbor.

"Oh, I know myself," says little Fairly, for he was as cute as a fox, as I said before, and wouldn't tell his saycrets to a stone wall, let alone a companion. And what do you think he done wid the hide? Guess now—throth I'd let you guess from this to Christmas, and you'd never come inside it. Faix it was the complatest thing ever you heerd. What would you think but he tuk the hide and cut six little holes an partic'lar places he knew av himself, and thin he goes and he gets his mother's fortin', the six shillin's I tould you about, and he hides the six shillin's in the six holes, and away he wint to a fair was convenient, about three days afther, where there was a sight o' people, and a power o' sellin' and buyin', and dhrinkin' and fightin', by course, *and why nat?*

Well, Fairly ups and he goes right into the very heart o' the fair, an' he spread out his hide to the greatest advantage, and he began to cry out (and by the same token, though he was little he had a mighty sharp voice and could be h'ard farther nor a bigger man) well he began to

cry out, "Who wants to buy a hide?–the *rale* hide—the ould original
goolden bull's hide that kem from furrin parts—who wants to make
their fortin' now?"

"What do you ax for your hide?" says a man to him.

"Oh, I only want a thrifle for it," says Fairly, "seein' I'm disthressed
for money, at this present writin'", says he, "and by fair or foul manes
I must rise the money," says he, "at wanst, for if I could wait, it's not
the thrifle I'm axin' now I'd take for the hide."

"By gor you talk," says the man, "as if the hide was worth the
King's ransom, and I'm thinkin' you must have a great want of a few
shillin's," says he, "whin the hide is all you have to the fore, to dipind
an."

"Oh, that's all *you* know about it," says Fairly, "shillin's indeed; by
gor it's handfuls o' money the hide is worth. Who'll buy a hide—the
rale goolden bull's hide!!!"

"What do you ax for your hide?" says another man.

"Only a hundher guineas." says Fairly.

"A hundher what?" says the man.

"A hundher guineas," says Fairly.

"Is it takin' lave of your siven small sinses you are?" says the man.

"Why thin indeed I b'lieve I am takin' lave o' my sinses sure
enough," says Fairly, "to sell my hide so chape."

"Chape," says the man, "arrah thin listen to the little mad vagabone," says he to the crowd, that was gother about by this time, "listen
to him askin' a hundher guineas for a hide."

"Aye," says Fairly, "and the well laid out money it'ill be to whoever
has the luck to buy it. This is none o' your common hides—it's the
goolden bull's hide—the Pope's goolden bull's hide, that kem from
furrin parts, and it's a fortune to whoever'ill have patience to bate his
money out iv it."

"How do you mane?" says a snug ould chap, that was always
poachin' about for bargains—"I never heard of batin' money out of a
hide," says he.

"Well, then, I'll show you," says Fairly, "and only I'm disthressed
for a hundher guineas, that I must have before Monday next," says he,
"I wouldn't part wid this hide; for every day in the week you may
thrash a fistful o' shillin's out of iv it, if you take pains, as you may

see." And wid that, my jew'l, he ups wid a cudgel, he had in his hand, and he began leatherin' away at the hide; and he hits it *in the place he knew himself,* and out jump'd one o' the shillin's he hid there. "Hurroo!" says little Fairly, "darlint you wor, you never desaived me yet!!" and away he thrashed again, and out jumped another shillin'. "That's your sort!" says Fairly, "the devil a sitch wages any o' yiz ever got for thrashin' as this—and then another whack, and away wid another shillin'.

"Stop, stop!" says the ould cravin' chap, "I'll give you the money for the hide," says he, "if you'll let me see can I bate money out iv it." And wid that he began to thrash the hide, and, of course, another shillin' jumped out.

"Oh! it's yourself has the rale twist in your elbow for it," says Fairly; "and I see by that same, that you're above the common, and desarvin' of my favor."

Well, my dear, at the word *"desarvin' o' my favor,"* the people that was gother round, (for by this time all the fair a'most was there), began to look into the rights o' the thing, and, one and all, they agreed that little Fairly was one o' the *"good people";* for if he wasn't a fairy, how could he do the like? and, besides, he was sitch a dawnshee craythur they thought what else could he be? and says they to themselves, "That ould divil, Mulligan, it's the likes iv him id have the luck iv it; and let alone all his gains in *this* world, and his scrapin' and screwin', and it's the fairies themselves must come to help him, as if he wasn't rich enough before." Well, the ould chap paid down a hundher guineas in hard goold to little Fairly, and off he wint wid his bargain.

"The divil do you good wid it," says one, grudgin' it to him.

"What business has he wid a hide?" says another, jealous of the ould fellow's luck.

"Why nat?" says another, "sure he'd shkin a flint any day, and why wouldn't he shkin a cow?"

Well, the owld codger wint home as plased as Punch wid his bargain; and indeed little Fairly had no raison not to be satisfied, for, in throth, he got a good price for the hide, considherin' the markets wasn't so high thin as they are now, by rayson of the staymers, that *makes gintlemen av the pigs,* sendin' them an their thravles to furrin parts, so that a rasher o'bacon in poor Ireland is gettin' scarce even on a Aisther Sunday.[3]

You may be sure the poor owld mother of little Fairly was proud enough whin she seen him tumble out the hard goold an the table forninst her, and "my darlint you wor," says she, "an' how did you come by that sight o' goold?"

"I'll tell you another time," says little Fairly, "but you must set off to my brother's now, and ax him to lind me the loan av his scales."

"Why, what do you want wid a scales, honey?" says the owld mother.

"Oh! I'll tell you *that* another time too," says little Fairly, "but be aff now, and don't let the grass grow undher your feet."

Well, off wint the owld woman, and maybe you'd want to know yourself what it was Fairly wanted wid the scales. Why, thin, he only wanted thim just for to make big Fairly curious about the matther, that he might play him a thrick, as you'll see by-an-by.

Well, the little owld woman wasn't long in bringin' back the scales, and whin she gave them to little Fairly, "There, now," says he, "sit down beside the fire, and there's a new pipe for you, and a quarther o' tobaccy, that I brought home for you from the fair, and do you make yourself comfortable," says he, "till I come back"; and out he wint, and sat down behind a ditch, to watch if big Fairly was comin' to the house, for he thought the curosity o' the big gommoch and the garran more would make them come down to spy about the place, and see what he wanted wid the scales; and, sure enough, he wasn't there long when he seen them both crassin' a style hard by, and in he jumped into the gripe o' the ditch, and run along under the shelter o' the back av it, and whipped into the house, and spread all his goold out an the table, and began to weigh it in the scales.

But he wasn't well in, whin the cord o' the latch was dhrawn, and in marched big Fairly, and the garran more, his mother, without "by your lave," or "God save you," for they had no breedin' at all.[4] Well,

---

3. *On Easter Sunday, in Ireland, whoever is not proscribed, by the dire edicts of poverty, from the indulgence, has a morsel of meat, as a bonne bouche after the severe fasting in Lent, enjoined by the Roman Catholic Church.*

4. *Good manners.*

my jewel, the minit they clapped their eyes an the goold, you'd think the sight id lave their eyes; and indeed not only their eyes, let alone, but their tongues in their heads was no use to thim, for the divil a word either o' them could spake for beyant a good five minutes. So, all that time, little Fairly kept never mindin' them, but wint an a weighin' the goold, as busy as a nailor, and at last, whin the big brute kem to his speech, "Why, thin," says he, "what's that I see you doin?" says he.

"Oh, it's only divartin' myself I am," says little Fairly, "thryin' what woight o' goold I got for my goods at the fair," says he.

"Your goods indeed," says the big chap, "I suppose you robbed some honest man an the road, you little vagabone," says he.

"Oh, I'm too little to rob any one," says little Fairly. I'm not a fine big able fellow, *like you,* to *do that same."*—"Thin how did you come by the goold?" says the big savage—"I towld you before, by sellin' my goods," says the little fellow.—"Why, what goods have *you,* you poor unsignified little brat?" says big Fairly, "you never had any thing but your poor beggarly cow, and she's dead."

"Throth, then, she is dead; and more by token, 'twas yourself done for her, complate, anyhow; and I'm beholden to you for that same, the longest day I have to live, for it was the makin' o' me. You wor ever and always *the good brother to me;* and never more than whin you killed my cow, for it's the makin' o' me. The divil a rap you see here I'd have had if my cow was alive, for I wint to the fair to sell her hide, brakin' my heart to think that it was only a poor hide I had to sell, and wishin' it was a cow was to the fore; but, my dear, whin I got there, there was no ind to the demand for hides, and the divil a one, good, bad, or indifferent, was there but my own, and there was any money for hides, and so I got a hundher guineas for it, and there they are."

"Why thin do you tell me so?" says the big chap.

"Divil a lie in it," says little Fairly—"I got a hundher guineas for the hide." Oh, I wish I had another cow for you to kill for me,—throth would I!"

"Come home, mother," says big Fairly, without sayin' another word, and away he wint home, and what do you think he done but he killed every individyal cow he had, and "By gor," says he, "it's the rich man I'll be when I get a hundher guineas apiece for all their hides," and accordingly off he wint to the next fair, hard by, and he brought a carload o' hides, and began to call out in the fair, "Who wants the hides?—here's the chape hides—only a hundher guineas apiece!"

"Oh do you hear that vagabone that has the assurance to come chatin' the country again?" says some people that was convaynient, and that heerd o' the doin's at the other fair, and how the man was chated by a *sleeveen* vagabone—"and think of him, to have the impudence to come *here*, so nigh the place to take in *uz* now! But we'll be even wid him," says they; and so they went up to him, and says they to the thievin' roguc, "Honest man," says they, "what's that you have to sell?"

"Hides," says he.

"What do you ax for them?" says they.

"A hundher and ten guineas apiece," says he—for he was a greedy crathur, and thought he never could have enough.

"Why you riz the price on them since the last time," says they.

"Oh these are better," says big Fairly; "but I don't mind if I sell them for a hundher apiece, if you give me the money down," says he.

"You shall be ped an the spot," says they—and with that they fell an him, and thrash'd him like a *shafe,* till they didn't lave a *spark* o' sinse in him, and then they left him sayin', *"Are you ped now, my boy!* — faix you'll be a warnin' to all rogues for the futhur, how they come to fairs, chatin' honest min out o' their money, wid cock-and-bull stories about their hides—but in throth I think your own hide isn't much better of the tannin' it got today—faix an' it was the rale *oak bark* was put to it, and that's the finest tan stuff in the world, and I think it'ill sarve you for the rest o' your life."—And with that they left him for dead.

But you may remark, it's hardher to kill a dirty noxious craythur than any thing good,—and so by big Fairly—he conthrived to get home, and his vagabone mother sawdhered him up afther a manner, and the minit he was come to his sthrenth at all, he detarmint to be revenged on little Fairly for what he had done, and so off he set to catch him while he'd be at brekquest, and he bowlted into the cabin wid a murtherin' shillely in his fist—and "Oh," says he, "you little mischievous miscrayant," says he, "what made you ruinate me by makin' me kill my cows?" says he.

"Sure I didn't bid you kill your cows," says little Fairly—and that was all thrue, for you see, *there* was the cuteness o' the little chap, for he didn't *bid* him kill them sure enough, but he *let an* in that manner, that deludherd the big fool, and sure divil mind him.

"Yes, you did bid me," says big Fairly, "or all as one as bid me, and I haven't a cow left, and my bones is bruk all along o' your little jackeen *manyewvers,* you onlooky sprat that you are, but by this and that I'll have my revinge o' you now," and with that he fell an him and was goin' to murther poor little Fairly, only he run undher a stool, and kept tiggin' about from one place to th' other, that the big botch couldn't get a right offer at him at all at all, and at last the little owld mother got up to put a stop to the ruction, but if she did, my jew'l, it was the unlooky minit for her, for by dad she kem in for a chance tap o' the cudgel that big Fairly was weltin' away with, and you know there's an owld sayin', "a chance shot may kill the divil," and why not an owld woman?

Well, that put an end to the *skrimmage,* for the phillilew that little Fairly set up whin he seen his owld mother kilt, would ha' waked the dead, and the big chap got frekened himself, and says little Fairly, "By gor, if there's law to be had," says he, "and I think *I have* a chance o' justice, *now that I have money to spare,* and, if there's law in the land, I'll have you in the body o' the jail afore tomorrow," says he; and wid that the big chap got cowed, and wint off like a dog without his tail, and so poor little Fairly escaped bein' murthered that offer, and was left to cry over his mother, an' indeed the craythur was sorry enough, and he brought in the neighbors and gev the ould woman a dacent wake, and there was few pleasanther evenin's that night in the country than the same wake, for Fairly was mighty fond of his mother, and faix he done the thing ginteely by her, and good raison he had, for she was the good mother to him while she was alive, and by dad, by his own cuteness, he conthrived she should be the useful mother to him after she was dead too. For what do you think he done? Oh! by the Piper o' Blessintown you'd never guess, if you wor guessin' from this to Saint Tib's eve, and that falls neither before nor afther Christmas we all know. Well, there's no use guessin', so I must tell you. You see the ould mother was a nurse to the Squire that lived hard by, and so, by coorse, she had a footin' in the house any day in the week she pleased,

and used often to go over to see the Squire's children, for she was as
fond o' them a'most as if she nursed *thim* too; and so what does Fairly
do but he carried over the ould mother, stiff as she was, and dhressed
in her best, and he stole in, *unknownst,* into the Squire's garden, and he
propped up the dead ould woman stan'in' hard by a well was in the
gardin, wid her face forninst the gate, and her back to the well, and
wid that he wint into the house, and made out the childhre, and says
he, "God save you, Masther Tommy," says he, "God save you, Masther
Jimmy, Miss Matty, and Miss Molshee," says he, "an' I'm glad to see
you well, and sure there's the ould Mammy nurse come to see yiz,
childhre," says he, "and she's down by the well in the garden, and she
has gingerbread for yiz," says he, "and whoever o' yiz runs to her
first'ill get the most gingerbread; and I'd rekimmind yiz to lose no
time but run a race and sthrive who'll win the gingerbread." Well, my
dear, to be sure off set the young imps runnin' and screechin', "Here I
am, mammy nurse, here I am," and they wor brakin' their necks
a'most, to see wh'd be there first, and wid that, they run wid sitch
voylence, that the first o' thim run whack up agin the poor ould
woman's corpse, and threwn it over plump into the middle o' the well.
To be sure the childhre was frekened, as well they might, and back
agin they ran, as fast as they kem, roarin' murther, and they riz the
house in no time, and little Fairly was among the first to go see what
was the matther, (by the way) and he set up a *hullagone* my jewel that
ud split the heart of a stone; and out kem the Squire and his wife, and
"What's the mather?" says they. "Is it what's the matther" says Fairly,
"don't yiz see my lovely ould mother is dhrowned by these devil's
imps o' childhre?" says he. "Oh Master Jimmy, is that the way you
thrated the poor ould mammy nurse, to go dhrowned her like a *rat*
afther that manner?"

"Oh, the childhre didn't intind it," says the Squire.
"I'm sorry for your mother, Fairly, but—"
"But what?" says little Fairly, "sorry—in throth and I'll make you
sorry, for I'll rise the counthry, or I'll get justice for sitch an unnath'ral
murther; and whoever done it must go to jail, if it was even Miss
Molshee herself."

Well the Squire did not like the matther to go to that, and so says
he, "Oh, I'll make it worth your while so say nothing about it, Fairly,

and here's twenty goolden guineas for you," says he.

"Why thin do you think me such a poor-blooded craythur, as to sell my darlin' ould mother's life for twenty guineas? No in throth, tho' if you wor to make it fifty I might be talkin' to you."

Well, the Squire thought it was a dear mornin's work, and that he had very little for his money in a dead ould woman, but sooner than have the childhre get into trouble and have the matther made *a blowin' horn* of, he gev him the fifty guineas, and the ould mother was dhried and waked over agin, so that she had greater respect ped to her than a Lord or a Lady. So you see what cleverness and a *janius* for cuteness does.

Well, away he wint home afther the ould woman was buried, wid his fifty guineas snug in his pocket, and so he wint to big Fairly's to ax for the loan of the scales once more, and the brother ax'd him for what. "Oh, it's only a small thrifle more o' goold I have," says the little chap, "that I want to weigh."

"Is it *more* goold?" says big Fairly, "why it's a folly to talk, but you must be either a robber or a coiner to come by money so fast."

"Oh, this is only a thrifle I kem by the death o' my mother," says little Fairly.

"Why bad luck to the rap *she* had to lave you, any way," says the big chap.

"I didn't say she left me a fortin'," says little Fairly.

"You said you kem by the money by your mother's death," says the big brother.

"Well, an' that's thrue," says the little fellow, "an' I'll tell you how it was. You see, afther you killed her, I thought I might as well make the most I could of her, and says I to myself, faix and I had great luck wid the cow he killed for me, and why wouldn't I get more for my mother nor a cow? and so away I wint to the town, and I offered her to the docthor there, and he was greatly taken wid her, and by dad he wouldn't let me lave the house without sellin' her to him, and faix he gev me fifty guineas for her."

"Is it fifty guineas for a corpse?"

"It's thruth I'm tellin' you, and was much obleeged into the bargain, and the raison is, you see, that there's no sitch thing to be had, for love or money, as a dead ould woman—there's no killin' them at

all at all, so that a dead ould woman is quite a curosity."

"Well, there's the scales for you," says big Fairly, and away the little chap wint to weigh his goold (as he let on) as he did before. But what would you think, my dear—throth you'll hardly b'lieve me whin I tell you. Little Fairly hadn't well turned his back, whin the big savage wint into the house where his ould mother was and tuck up a rapin' hook, and kilt her an the spot—divil a lie in it. Oh, no wondher you look cruked at the thoughts of it; but it's morially thrue,—faix he cut the life out iv her, and he determined to turn in his harvist, for that same, as soon as he could, and so away he wint to the docthor in the town hard by, where little Fairly towld him he sowld *his* mother, and he knocked at the door and walked into the hall with a sack on his shouldher, and settin' down the sack, he said he wanted to spake to the docthor. Well, when the docthor kem, and heerd the vagabone talkin' of fifty guineas for an owld woman, he began to laugh at him; but whin he opened the sack, and seen how the poor owld craythur was murthered, he set up a shout. "Oh, you vagabone," says he, "you sack-im-up villain!" says he, "you've Burked the woman," says he, "and now you come to *rape* the fruits o' your *murdher.*" Well, the minit big Fairly heerd the word *murdher,* and *rapin'* the reward, he thought the docthor was up to the way of it, and he got frekened, and with that the docthor opened the hall-door and called the watch, but Fairly bruk loose from him, and ran away home; and when once he was gone, *the docthor thought there would be no use in rising a ruction* about it, and so he shut the door, and never minded the police. Big Fairly, to be sure, was so frekened, he never cried stop, antil he got clean outside the town, and with that, the first place he wint to was little Fairly's house, and, burstin' in the door, he said, in a tarin' passion, "What work is this you have been at now, you onlooky miscrayint?" says he.

"I haven't been at any work," says little Fairly. "See, yourself," says he, "*my sleeves is new,*" says he, howldin' out the cuffs av his coat to him at the same time, to show him.

"Don't think to put me aff that-a-way with your little kimmeens, and your divartin' capers," says the big chap, "for I tell you I'm in airnest, and it's no jokin' matther it'ill be to you, for, by this an' that, I'll have the life o' you, you little *spidhogue* of an abortion, as you are, you made me kill my cows. Don't say a word, for you know it's thrue."

"I never made you kill your cows," says little Fairly, no ways danted by the fierce looks o' the big bosthoon.

"Whisht! you vagabone!" says the big chap. "You didn't bid me do it, out o' the face, in plain words, but you made me sinsible."

"Faix, an' that was doin' a wondher," says little Fairly, who couldn't help havin' the laugh at him, though he was sore afeard.

"Bad luck to you, you little sneerin' vagabone," says the big chap again, "I know what you mane, you long headed schkamer, that you are; but by my sowl, your capers'ill soon be cut short, as you'll see to your cost. But, before I kill you, I'll show you, to your face, the villain that you are, and it is no use your endayvourin' to consale your bad manners to me, for if you had a veil as thick as the shield of A–jax, which was made o' siv'n bull hides, it would not sarve for to cover the half o' your inni–quitties."[5]

"Whoo! that's the ould schoolmasther's speech you're puttin' an us now," says little Fairly, "and faith it's the only thin you iver larned, I b'lieve, from him."

"Yis, I larned how fine a thing it is to whop a little chap less than myself, and you'll see, with a blessin', how good a scholar I am at that same; and you desarve it, for I towld you just now, before you intherrupted me, how you made me kill all my cows, (and that was the sore loss), and afther that, whin you could do no more, you made me kill my mother, and divil a good it done me, but nigh hand got me into the watch-house; and so now I'm detarmint you won't play me any more thricks, for I'll hide you, snug, in the deepest boghole, in the Bog of Allen, and if you throuble me afther that, faix I think it 'ill be the wondher"; and, with that he made a grab at the little chap, and while you'd be sayin' "thrap stick," he cotch him, and put him, body and bones, into a sack, and he thrown the sack over the back of a horse was at the door, and away he wint in a tarin' rate, straight for the Bog of Allen. Well, to be sure, he couldn't help stoppin' at a public-house, by the road side, *for he was dhry, with the rage;* an' he tuk the sack where little Fairly was tied up, and he lifted it aff o' the horse, an' put it standin' up beside the door goin' into the public-house; and he wasn't well gone in, whin a farmer was comin' by too, and he was as dhry

5. *A lady assured me of this as the genuine speech of a hedge schoolmaster.*

wid the dust, as ever big Fairly was with the rage, (an' indeed it's wondherful how aisy it is to make a man dhry); and so, as he was goin' in, he sthruck agin the sack that little Fairly was in, and little Fairly gev a groan that you'd think kem from the grave; and says he (from inside o' the sack), "God forgive you," says he.

"Who's there?" says the farmer, startin', and no wondher.

"It's me," says little Fairly, "and may the Lord forgive you," says he, "for you have disturbed me, and I *half-way to heaven.*"

"Why, who are you at all?" says the farmer. "Are you a man?" says he.

"I am a man now," says little Fairly, "though, if you didn't disturb me, I'd have been an angel of glory in less than no time," says he.

"How do you make that out, honest man?" says the farmer.

"I can't explain it to you," says little Fairly, "*for it's a mystery;* but what I tell you is thruth," says he, "and I tell you that, whoever is in this sack at this present," says he, "is as good as half-way to heav'n, and indeed I thought I was there, a'most, only you sthruck agin me, an' disturbed me."

"An' do you mane for to say," says the farmer, "that whoiver is in that sack will go to heaven?"

"Faix, they are on their road there, at all events," says little Fairly, "and if they lose their way, it's their own fault."

"Oh thin," says the farmer, "maybe you'd let me get into the sack along wid you, for to go to heaven too."

"Oh, the horse that's to bring us *doesnt carry double*," says little Fairly.

"Well, will you let me get into the sack instead iv you?" says the farmer.

"Why, thin, do you think I'd let any one take sitch a dirty advantage o' me as to go to heaven afore me?" says little Fairly.

"Oh, I'll make it worth your while," says the farmer.

"Why, thin, will you ontie the sack," says little Fairly, "and jist let me see who it is that has the impidince to ax me to do the like." And with that, the farmer ontied the sack, and little Fairly popped out his head. "Why, thin, do you think," says he, "that a hangin'-gone lookin' thief, *like you,* has a right to go to heaven afore me?"

"Oh," says the farmer, "I've been a wicked sinner in my time, and I haven't much longer to live; and, to tell you the thruth, I'd be glad to get to heaven in that sack, if it's thrue what you tell me."

"Why," says little Fairly, "don't you know it is my *sackcloth and ashes* that the faithful see the light o' glory?"

"Thrue for you indeed," says the farmer. "Oh murther, let me get in there, and I'll make it worth your while."

"How do you make that out?" says little Fairly.

"Why, I'll give you five hundher guineas," says the farmer, "and I think that's a power o' money."

"But what's a power o' money compared to heaven?" says little Fairly; "and do you think I'd sell my sowl for five hundher guineas?"

"Well, there's five hundher more in an owld stockin', in the oak box, in the cabin by the crass-roads, at Dhrumsnookie, for I am owld Tims o' Dhrumsnookie, and you'll inherit all I have, if you consint."

"But what's a thousand guineas compared to heaven?" says little Fairly.

"Well, do you see all them heads o' cattle there?" says the farmer. "I have just dhruv them here from Ballinasloe," says he, "and every head o' cattle you see here, shall be yours also, if you let me into that sack, that I may go to heaven instead o' you."

"Oh think o' my poor little soul," says Fairly.

"Tut, man," says the farmer, "I've twice as big a sowl as you; and besides, I'm owld, and you're young, and I have no time to spare, and you may get absolution aisy, and make your pace in good time."

"Well," says little Fairly, "I feel for you," says he, "an' I'm half inclined to let you overpersuade me to have your will o' me."

"That's a jewel," says the farmer.

"But make haste," says little Fairly, "for I don't know how soon you might get a refusal."

"Let me in at wanst," says the farmer. So, my dear, Fairly got out, and the farmer got in, and the little chap tied him up; and says he to the farmer, "There will be great *norations* made agin you, all the way you're goin' along; and you'll hear o' your sins over and over agin, and you'll hear o' things you never done at all," says little Fairly, "but never say a word, or you won't go where I was goin'. Oh! why did I let you persuade me?"

"Lord reward you!" says the poor farmer.

"And your conscience will be sthreckin' you all the time," says little Fairly; "and you'll think a'most it's a stick is sthrekin' you, but you mustn't let an, nor say a word, but pray *inwardly* in the sack."

"I'll not forget," says the farmer.

"Oh! you"ll be reminded of it," says Fairly, "for you've a bad conscience I know; and the seven deadly sins will be goin' your road, and keepin' you company, and every now and then they'll be *puttin' their comether* an you, and callin' you 'brother,' but don't let on to know them at all, for they'll be mislaydin' you, and just do you keep quite [quiet] and *you'll see the ind iv it.*" Well, just at that minit little Fairly heerd big Fairly comin', and away he run and hid inside iv a churn was dhryin' at the ind o' the house; and big Fairly lifted the sack was standin' at the door, and feelin' it more weighty nor it was before, he said, "Throth, I think you're growin' heavy with grief; but here goes, any how," and, with that, he hoist it up on the horse's back, an' away he wint to the Bog iv Allen.

Now, you see, big Fairly, like every blackguard that has the bad blood in him, the minit he had the sup o' dhrink in, the dirty turn kem out: and so, as he wint along he began to wallop the poor baste, and the sack where his little brother was (as he thought, the big fool), and to gibe, and jeer him for his divarshin. But the poor farmer did as little Fairly towld him, an' never a word he said at all, though he couldn't help roaring out every now and thin, whin he felt the soft ind of big Fairly's shillelah across his backbone; and sure the poor fool thought it was his bad conscience and the seven deadly sins was tazin' him; but he wouldn't answer a word for all that, though the big savage was *aggravatin'* him every fut o' the road antil they kem to the bog; and whin he had him there, faix he wasn't long in choosin' a boghole for him—and, my jew'l, in he popped the poor farmer nick and heels, sack and all; and as the soft bog stuff and muddy wather closed over him, "I wish you a safe journey to the bottom, young man," says the big brute, grinnin' like a cat at a cheese, "and as clever a chap as you are, I don't think you'll come back out o' that in a hurry; and it's throubled I was wid you long enough, you little go-the-ground schkamer, but I'll have a quiet life for the futhur." And wid that he got up an his horse, and away he wint home; but he had not gone over a mile, or there-away, whin who should he see but little Fairly mounted on the farmer's horse, dhrivin' the biggest dhrove o' black cattle you ever seen; and, by dad, big Fairly grewn as white as a sheet whin he clapt his eyes an him, for he thought it was not himself at all was in it, but his ghost; and he was goin' to turn and gallop off, whin little Fairly called out to him to stay, for that he wanted to speak to him. So whin he seen it was himself, he wondhered, to be sure, and small blame to him—and says he, "Well, as cute as I knew you wor, by gor, this last turn o' yours bates Bannagher—and how the divil are you here at all, whin I thought you wor cuttin' turf wid your sharp little nose, in the Bog of Allen? for I'll take my affidowndavy, I put you into the deepest hole in it, head foremost not half an hour agon."

"Throth you did, sure enough," says little Fairly, "and you wor ever and always the good brother to me, as I often said before, but by dad, you never done rightly for me antil today, but you made me up now in airnest."

"How do you mane?" says big Fairly.

"Why, do you see all this cattle here I'm dhrivin'?" says little Fairly.

"Yes I do, and whose cattle are they?"

"They're all my own—every head o' them."

"An' how did you come by them?"

"Why you see, when you threwn me into the boghole, I felt it mighty cowld at first, and it was mortial dark, and I felt myself goin' down and down, that I thought I'd never stop sinking, and wondhered if there was any bottom to it at all, and at last I began to feel it growin' warm, and pleasant, and light, and whin I kem to the bottom, there was the loveliest green field you ever clapped your eyes on, and thousands upon thousands o' cattle feedin' and the grass so heavy that they wor up to their ears in it—it's thruth I'm tellin' you—O, divil sitch meadows I ever seen, and whin I kem to myself, for indeed I was rather surprised, and thought it was dhramin' I was—whin I kem to myself, I was welkim'd by a very ginteel spoken little man, the dawnshiest craythur you ever seen, by dad I'd have made six iv him, myself, and says he, 'You're welkim to the undher story o' the Bog iv Allen, Fairly.'—'Thank you kindly, sir,' says I.—'And how is all wid you?' says he.—'Hearty indeed,' says I.—'And what brought you here?' says he.—'My big brother,' says I.—'That was very good iv him,' says he.—'Thrue for you, sir' says I. 'He is always doin' me a good turn,' says I.—'Oh then he never done you half so good a turn as this,' says he; 'for you'll be the richest man in Ireland soon.'—'Thank you, sir,' says I; 'but I don't see how.'—'Do you see all them cattle grazin' there?' says he.—'To be sure I do,' says I. 'Well,' says he, 'take as many o' them as your heart desires, and bring them home wid you.'—'Why sure,' says I, 'how could I get back, myself, up out of the boghold, let alone dhraggin' bullocks afther me?'—'Oh,' says he, 'the way is aisy enough, for you have nothin' to do but dhrive them out the back way over there,' says he, pointin' to a gate. And sure enough, my darlint, I got all the bastes you see here, and dhruv them out, and here I am goin' home wid 'em, and maybe I won't be the rich man—av coorse I geve the best o' thanks to the little owld man, and gev him the hoighth o' good language for his behavor. And with that, says he, 'You may come back again, and take the rest o' them,' says he —and faix sure enough I'll go back the minit I get these bastes home, and have another turn out o' the boghole."

"Faix and I'll be before hand wid you," says big Fairly.

"Oh, but you shan't," says little Fairly; "it was I discovered the place, and why shouldn't I have the good iv it?"

"You greedy little hound," say the big fellow, "I'll have my share o' them as well as you." And with that he turned about his horse, and away he galloped to the boghole, and the little fellow galloped afther him, purtendin' to be in a desperate fright afeard the other would get there first, and he cried "Stop the robber!" afther him, and whin he came to the soft place in the bog, they both lit, and little Fairly got before the big fellow, and purtended to be makin' for the boghole in a powerful hurry, cryin' out as he passed him, "I'll win the day! I'll win the day!" and the big fellow pulled fut afther him as hard as he could, and hardly a puff left in him he run to that degree, and he was afeared that little Fairly would bate him and get all the cattle, and he was wishin' for a gun that he might shoot him, whin the cute little divil, just as he kem close to the edge o' the boghole, *let an* that his fut slipped and he fell down, cryin' out, "Fair play! fair play!—wait till I rise!" but the words wasn't well out of his mouth whin the big fellow kem up. "Oh, the divil a wait," says he, and he made one desperate dart at the boghole, and jumped into the middle of it. "Hurroo!!" says little

Fairly, gettin' an his legs agin and runnin' over to the edge o' the boghole, and just as he seen the great splaw feet o' the big savage sinkin' into the sludge, he called afther him, and says he, "I say, big Fairly, don't take all the cattle, but lave a thrifle for me. *I'll wait, however, till you come back,*" says the little rogue, laughin' at his own cute conthrivance, "and I think now I'll lade a quiet life," says he; and with that he wint home, and from that day out he grewn richer and richer every day, and was the greatest man in the whole counthry side; and all the neighbors gev in to him that he was the most knowledgable man in thim parts, but they all thought it was quare that his name should be *Fairly,* for it was agreed, one and all, *that he was the biggest rogue out,*—barrin' Balfe, the robber.

His Magnificence
Shan F. Bullock

WHEN HIS MAGNIFICENCE stepped from the train upon the dingy little platform of Bunn Station, the porter, the station-master, the car-driver from the Diamond Hotel, the loiterers, the passengers, all did him reverence. His like or equal had not met their gaze for many a day. He had the bearing and appearance of a prince. His luggage was powerful. The battered train that had carried him, the paltry station that received him, the yokels who eyed him, by very contrast, seemed to shrink back ashamed. It was America herself set off against old Ireland.

"Who is he at all?" whispered one of the flurried, heated porter.

"Ach, g'luck an' don't bother me!" replied the porter. "How the divil can I tell?"

The car-driver, having an eye to business, stole to the pile of baggage and spelled out the name on a label: 'THOMAS BURKE, ESQ.' He read, whistled, stole back, and spread the news.

"It's Tommy Burke," said one to another; "Tommy Burke home from the States—begob!"

The news, to the admirers of His Magnificence, brought a sense of relief if not of disappointment. He was no potentate, then, after all. Sure they knew the man; he was only one of themselves; sure they minded the day he went; didn't he come from Gorteen over there? Wasn't his ould mother and his brother James living there in the ould place still? Ay! But who'd have thought it; for his kind never did much good in the world. Powerful, powerful! Sure it's a grand country. Ay!

"It's an ojus pile, y'ur honor," said the porter, touching his cap. "Ye'll want a car?"

The car-driver stepped forward.

"There's one outside, sur, from the hotel, sur," said he. "Mebbe ye'd be wantin' to put up?"

His Magnificence eyed the two loftily.

"Yaas," drawled he, and looked at the baggage; "yaas—reckon it'll want movin'." He waved his hand. "Send it on; send it on—you'll see the address. Naw, naw, Jehu; naw, naw, I want none o' your tarnation hearses. Reckon I'll foot it."

The crowd divided. His Magnificence condescended to walk. The crowd closed in behind him, followed him through the station, past the hotel car, and up the slope towards Bunn town.

Already the word had spread. Bunn was out, waiting, watching, shouting the news.

"Here he is! Be the Holy! Look at the watch-chain on him! *An'* the rings! Och, an' the clothes av him! An' that's Tommy Burke? Aw now, now! Sure it's wonderful—sure it's an ojus country for money—ay! ay!"

Tommy, as he leisurely marched up the street pretending a profound interest in the houses and shops, took his reception calmly. He had reckoned upon making an impression. It was his due. He heard his name whispered as he passed, heard the criticisms on his raiment and appearance, saw the faces right and left at the doors before him, and heard the swelling chorus of comment behind as Bunn left the doors, spread across the street, and gave play to its tongue and excitement. It was hid due. Everyone knew him; all had heard of his success in Chicago. It was natural. But *he*? He knew no one. He had forgotten everyone. Phew! the stink—that darned turf smoke. Such a God-forsaken hole of a town!—rags, dirt, laziness. Think of Chicago and think of Bunn! Why, he himself could buy out the whole place neck and crop. What pavements! What littered streets—pigs, fowls, dogs, dirty brats, women, men! What stores—merciful heavens!

Really His Magnificence might well have been less critical: not very many years had gone since the days when he himself, in rags and tatters, had hawked turf from door to door through that very street.

So His Magnificence, all glorious without, all scornful disgust within, marched on, past the market-house, down Bridge Street, over the big stone bridge—from which, had he cared to look, he would have seen the river tumbling gloriously among the boulders and rushing carelessly past a world of quiet beauty on its banks—went on along the road that leads to Gorteen; leaving Bunn excited behind him, and raising its voice in wonder that such a personage could allow himself to walk humbly through the dust.

"Ach," said Bunn, "sure he might ha' had a porter. Ah, but mebbe he doesn't want to be too grand goin' to the ould mother—ay, ay! Well, God speed him! But it's a power o' good some o' them fine rings an' chains 'd do the same mother—ah, now!"

His Magnificence was walking, first, because he wished to impress the natives along the way; and next, because he wanted to take stock, leisurely, of the half-forgotten country of his birth.

How did it compare with the land of wealth and freedom? H'm!—paltry, neglected, God-forsaken, thought His Magnificence. No enterprise, no capital, no anything—just the same as when he had left it, just the same. Little fields smothered all round with big hedges; rushes, whins, spade labor; marshes, bogs, naked wretched houses; struggling starved peasantry—these are what· he saw, these only. He had no eyes for the wild beauty of the hills crowding away towards his Majesty the mountain; for the peaceful wind of the stream flowing between the reeds and bulrushes, along meadows and fields, past the great pointed alders and the grazing cattle; the dappled blue sky above, and the rich-tinted earth below—how could Tommy have eyes for all this? He was a citizen, a hunter of the dollar; trade, pavements, smoke, dust, these were his kind: all that was nothing, mere poetical drivel, not worth the jingle of a cent.

Yet the country through which he was marching was the country of his birth; it had reared him well and given him a good start in health and brains. He might have condescended to look kindly on it, His Magnificence might, and to feel a little thrill of emotion as he came gradually on scenes and places which recalled his boyhood. He had done well away from the old country—it was none the worse for that; he had friends still lingering in its fields and homes; his old mother and his one brother were over there in Gorteen; it was not so bad that he did not care to come back to it, just for a holiday, to see his mother, to let people admire him and his, to—

A little white house, perched on the brow of a hill, away over Thrasna River in the land of Gorteen, caught his eye. He stopped dead; gazed at the house awhile; then, with his head down, walked on. *Bessie Darling,* he was thinking—*Bessie Darling,* is she there now, over there in that white cottage beyond Thrasna River?

He looked up again. How often he had gone up that hill; how often had he sat inside those white walls by the cheery hearthstone! *Bessie, Bessie*—he wondered how time and the world had used her. He was fond of her—once, he remembered. It was on this very road, he remembered, going home one day from Bunn fair—a little elated and reckless, because of Bunn whiskey, perhaps—that he had asked her to marry him. Had he asked her or only hinted? He forgot. Anyway he had promised at the parting to come back from America to fetch her. Well, he had come. Tommy Burke was ever a man of his word—he had come back faithful to his promise . . . . To fetch her? Ah! that was another matter. Circumstances had altered things . . . . Curious how she had dropped out of his mind! Once he had written, long ago; once she had written, long ago; then came work—work and success. Once or twice, years ago, he had thought of her—once or twice . . . . Where was she now? he wondered; had she forgotten him, or was she still waiting for him to come and fetch her? Oh! he hoped not. Suppose she were waiting over there for him; suppose she held him to his promise? Great Jupiter! Tommy Burke marry a lump of a country colleen! She used to be fair and sweet; half the country had been jealous of him. Yes, but that was years ago. What was she now? Bah! Absurd. She might go to Jerusalem. He could break his promise—yes, and pay for breaking it. Yes, siree!

He raised his head, and looking across the fields, tried to fall again into his old, complacent, critical groove. But, somehow, the effort did not succeed. His eyes would wander towards the white house on the hill. The name *Bessie* would sing in his ears. He foresaw possible trouble. The glory that had shone on him for a while in Bunn somehow shone no longer. No longer did he watch for the effect of his presence on the yokels who met him, nor half turn his head to catch a glimpse of their open-eyed stare as they turned to gaze after him. He stamped his foot on the stones.

"Damn it!" he said. "Why did I come back to this cursed country?"

He crossed Thrasna River and entered the land of Gorteen—that land of wisdom which eternally is honored in calling Tommy son. Here things took a better and more familiar aspect, and the spirits of Tommy became less of a burden. Bilboa, through which he had just passed—Pah! he remembered it was a nest of rebels; no wonder it was a wilderness. But Gorteen was fairer, and its people were children of loyalty and worth, if not of wealth. The cottages, here and there, with their gardens and orchards were pleasant to look upon; the hedges were often trim, the fields within them not a reproach. Poverty was everywhere; yes, poverty or next thing above it; still, it was not sluggards' poverty; there was everywhere signs of a patient struggle against adversity. But Tommy Burke was fast regaining his magnificence. He shook himself inside his well-filled raiment, mounted a ditch, and looked across the hedge at a field of young corn.

"Good Lord!" he said half aloud; "what is it at its best? Why do people stay on and struggle in this unfortunate country! Why can't they leave it, and do like me?"

He shook his head; it was inexplicable. Why had he left it? he thought. Brains, he answered, brains had led him. Why did his mother choose to stay on in it rather than come to him in America? He had asked her more than once—he did not choose to remember that the asking her was all he had ever done for her—why had she chosen to stay on there in poverty, living with his brother in their hut on their bit of wilderness? Old associations—love of the land? Ah! to glory with such talk . . . . He would have to sleep in that hut tonight, eat there— Ah! he would drive back and sleep in Bunn—

"Morra," came loudly across the road behind him; "that's a brave crop now."

The voice was familiar. His Magnificence turned: there, in a field across the road, stood big Ned Noble and his son James, leaning on their shovels and gazing curiously at him from the potato furrows.

"Why," said Ned, throwing down his shovel and starting forward wiping his palm on his breeches. "No!—begob it is! Arrah, how's yourself, Tommy, me boy? Welcim back, me son, to the ould country! Why, ye stand it rightly—begob! the best." He gave Tommy's hand a squeeze that made him wince. "Och, boys, oh boys!" Ned went on, "but you're changed!—not the same man at all, at all—dear, oh dear! Hoi, James. Come here, ye boy ye! Here's Tommy Burke back from the States."

James slouched out of his furrow, bashfully took Tommy's hand, and stood back, mutely admiring, whilst his father roared out the countryside news for the last five years and more—all who had died, who married, who changed farms, and so on.

"Ay, ay," said Ned, "powerful changes—powerful. But the ould mother beyant stands it rightly—aw the best. I needn't tellye, av coorse," Ned went on, looking sideways at Tommy, "that Bessie

Darlin' 's married—Eh? Ye didn't know? Well now, well now!—Aw
ay! married an' doin' well. An' ye didn't know? Sure I thought—"

His Magnificence turned the talk. The news was good; he could
have given Ned a dollar because of it; his heart was jumping; the sky
had cleared: still, he could not allow Ned Noble to be familiar or to
draw conclusions. He gave out, for quick circulation round the
countryside, a few facts about himself and his estate; set the mouth of
Ned's son James wider agape with a few observations on the glories of
Chicago; then, shook the clay from his boots and took again to the
road.

Ned and James went back to the potato furrows, learnt thoughtfully
on their shovels, and watched Tommy make his way up the *boreen* that
led to his mother's cottage.

"Jist to think o' that," said Ned, and shook his head; "rowlin' in
money, an' I mind the day ye could cont the ribs o' him through his
tatters! Man! James, did ye see yon watch-chain? Sure it's yon watch-
chain? Sure it's as thick as a cart tether—an' it's *goold!* An' the rings
av him! Och, och!"

"Ay," said James; "th' ould mother'll go daft over him—ay! I dunno
but mebbe Bessie Darlin' 'd better ha' waited a while afore marryin'—
ay!"

Ned turned and winked at James.

"You're right there, James," said he; "ay—an' d'ye mind the liar he
is, pretendin' he didn't know she was married! Couldn't I see he was
cut about it, him pullin' me up that short—troth, ay! Well, fire away at
that furrow; sure I must g' way home an' tell Mary the news."

Meanwhile His Magnificence was picking his way along the
boreen; not swearing very much at the ruts and the puddles; nor yet
letting his heart beat swiftly because of the surprise he was about to
spring on his old mother; not even raising his head that he might look
out over the fields or catch a glimpse of the home of his youth there in
front. Why should he look! Did he not know that the lane he was
stepping through, and the fields around him, and the house before him,
were just as they had ever been and just as they would ever remain?
Yes; and, for the rest, he was not walking with his thoughts?

Bessie's married, he kept thinking—*Bessie's married;* and his little
heart was glad. For the last time but one that day, he was His

Magnificence every inch of him. Trouble had fled. He could enjoy himself now; air his splendor about the country; do something for his people; betake himself to his own country when he felt so disposed. He thanked his maker Bessie was married.

How was it he had never heard? His brother had written once or twice, without saying anything. How was it? Oh, forgot perhaps—or felt that the news would be of no interest. She had been married for years, Ned said. For years? Ha! how soon she had forgotten him! Woman's constancy! Bah! *He* had not married—no! *He* had come back single—yes! And perhaps had she been single, and clean, and decent, and not vulgar, and had not gone off too much, he might – who knew? Ah! if she only knew—great Scott!—only *knew* what she had missed. Missed him; missed Chicago, and wealth, and position, and all the rest! If she only knew—yes, and she *should* know, soon too, what her hurry and promise-breaking had done for her. Yes, siree!

By this His Magnificence had steered himself safely up the *boreen,* and had passed the gate, just then lying wrecked on the ditch against the hedge, which on rare occasions had been known to keep goats and swine from invading the precincts of the home of all the Burkes. Was he magnificent still? Hardly. Twenty yards off was his old mother. Did his heart leap even now? Perhaps so; one thinks not.

He crossed the noisome tract which lay between the unsightliness of the byre on the one hand and the unsavoriness of the dunghill on the other, daintily stepped through the hens and ducks over the dirty puddled yard, and came to the door of his old home.

At the threshold he paused and looked around. Just the same—just the same—dirt, slatternliness, poverty—the Burkes were ever good-for-nothings. He was, he reflected, the only well-doer of them all. Pah!

He lifted the latch, and poked his head into the smoke.

"Mrs. Burke," he shouted. "Does Mrs. Burke live here?"

"Who's that?" came back, "Who are ye?"

"A stranger," said Tommy. "Are you Mrs. Burke?"

"Yis – yis," said his mother as she came towards the door. "Why—why—why—Ah God! ah God! it's Tommy – Ah me son, me son! Aw —aw—aw!"

The next moment a pair of old yellow arms were round His Magnificence, and willy-nilly he was dragged by the neck into the smoke and gloom of the home of his ancestors. Really, it served His Magnificence right.

One can hardly say that Tommy was happy as he sat one side of the hearthstone, in a straight-backed armchair, staring gloomily at the black tea-drawer boiling on the coals and the bacon frizzling on the pan—Oh, what a dinner! thought he—whilst his old mother held his hand, crooned over him, and by the score showered on him questions about himself and his welfare.

He answered dolefully, evasively; how could he answer otherwise, sitting in such a den, surrounded by such poverty, choked by such smoke, all the time very well aware that his splendor was down in the dirt—down in the dirt with his own mother, where he had been born, and where, all the years of his well-doing, he had suffered his mother to remain?

How could he talk freely to her of his wealth and his trade and his friends? His moral perception was not very delicate; but it served, just then, to give him the impression that to speak of these things was almost to reproach himself. Besides, she would not understand: better, perhaps, unfold his tale gradually. She was old and crotchety; perhaps —and God knows it was the basest thought Thomas Burke's little soul ever bred—she might reproach him, taunt him, point at hime and then at herself and mutter hard things about selfishness and ingratitude. How could he answer except dolefully and evasively?

Truly the day's passing was not bringing added splendor to His Magnificence.

Presently his mother let go his hand, and rose to get the dinner. Phew!—the smoke, the stuffiness, the gloom.

"Oh, for Heaven's sake, mother," he cried, "open the door, the window—anything, and give me air. I'll choke."

"Ah aisy, me son," said his mother, as she tottered towards the door, "aisy—whisht!—it's nothin'; it's only them fools o' turf, all wet they are. Come, sit over now, an' ate."

Tommy looked at the bare, littered table in disgust, and the strong coarse food thereon. His soul revolted; his manhood sickened; he gulped down a few mouthfuls; then, declaring he had no appetite, threw down his knife and fork, lit a cigar, and pulled his chair nearer the open door.

"You never sent me word about Bessie Darling's marriage, mother?" he said.

"Och no. Sure James wrote seldom; I forgot to tell him. How did ye find out?"

"H'm! Reckon ye didn't forget, mother. Who's the man? Any one I know?"

"Why, sure ye know? Didn't ye hear? Francy Phillips there beyant on the hill."

"Ah! Married long?"

"Och ay—this, this years an' years. Sure, she's four childer already. Tommy," his mother said, as she tottered forward and clutched his arm, "ye missed her well, dear. What'd the likes o' you, wi' all that property, do wi' the likes o' her? I was *rejoiced* to hear av her goin' – rejoiced, now. But sure ye niver cared much for her? Why should I tell ye?"

True, thought Tommy, true; why should he know? He had missed her well. Still, how soon she had forgotten him. Ah! if she only knew what *she* had missed. She should know; and at once.

"Yaas—no doubt—yaas," he replied to his mother. "Well, I reckon I'll take a look round. Go and see James perhaps. Find him in the fields, I suppose?"

Under pretence of going to see his brother, just then busy at the turf, Tommy crossed the fields, made a circuit of the bog, climbed a hill, and boldly opened the gate of Francis Phillips' garden.

The walk was trim, the flower-beds orderly, the cottage neat; he rapped at a green door with a brass knocker. He heard a sudden bustle inside, saw a face pressed for an instant against the parlor window: the door opened, and his old love stood before him.

Ah, thought His Magnificence, thank Heaven!

She was every inch an Irish farmer's wife—stout, bare-armed, fresh-complexioned, dressed in a loose bodice, a quilted petticoat, heavy boots, and wearing an old straw hat over her rough black hair.

"Good afternoon," said His Magnificence, as he raised his hat.

"Good evenin', sir,"

"Are you Mrs. Phillips?"

"Yes, sir,"

His Magnificence swelled himself.

"Aow—well, I'm Thomas Burke; just home from America, ye know."

Mrs. Phillips bit her lip, reddened a little, made a pluck at her apron; then put out her hand.

"Faith, an' you're welcim, Mr. Burke," said she. "Sorrow bit o' me knew ye at first. Sure it's good o' ye to come to see me. Come in, now, come in!"

She led the way—and as she went His Magnificence, at sight of the size and shape of her hob-nailed boots clattering along beneath her milk-stained petticoat, was not less thankful to Heaven for his deliverance from her well-worn charms—through the narrow earth-floored hall, just then heavy with smoke and kitchen odors, into the little earth-floored parlor, where the atmosphere struck close and smoky; dragged forward a chair, and asked him to sit down.

And this is Tommy, thought Bessie, as, pulling off her hat and seating herself before him, she let her eyes take in fully the details of his person—his jewelry, fine linen, fatness, grey hairs. Troth the world has used him well, thought she. What has he come for? To throw taunts at one, I suppose? Well, let him! Why did he go and leave me?

"Ye stand it well, Mr. Burke," said she. "But now you're odios changed. I widn't ha' known ye."

"Yaas," drawled His Magnificence; "reckon I am—it's a good while since you last saw me."

Ah; now it's coming, thought Bessie.

"Aw, 'deed it is," she said, "deed it is—years an' years. Here am I an ould married woman since that—ay, ay!"

She was giving His Magnificence every chance; better get it over, thought she.

"Yaas—heard about you from some one along the road, I think," drawled His Magnificence. "Congratulate you. Yaas, reckon I am changed, some. Not married myself—yet; but I've done some hard work since I left this country—left something considerable behind me when I started across the hearring-pond."

Bessie peered hard at him under her half-closed eyelids. She could not follow his drift. Isn't he going to say a word to me, thought she, about myself at all?

"Ah, yes," said she.

His Magnificence looked slowly all round the room—at the old yellow engravings in their wide walnut frames hanging against the damp-streaked walls; at the woolen antimacasars worked in orange and blue hanging over the painted chairs; at the flaring oleograph of King William over the mantelpiece, flanked on either side by dim old photographs in metal frames; at the artificial flowers on the big Bible on the table; at the half-open cupboard, inside which stood a whisky bottle among the best crockery-ware; at the geraniums in the window-recess—Lord! what vulgarity, he thought.

He looked at Bessie; and behind his eyes she saw scornful disgust.

"You've a pretty place here, I guess, Mrs. Phillips," he said, and waved his jeweled hand.

"Ah, now," said she, "not so bad, thank God—sure I could ha' been worse. But it's a poor place to sit the likes o' *you*, Mr. Burke; sure ye can't be well used to it, now?"

"Naw," replied His Magnificence, "p'raps not. I reckon in Chicago city I've a fine house and plenty in it. My furniture and fixings I calc'late would work out to a pretty high figure. My pictures an' statoos cost me, I guess, some hundreds of dollars. Two domestics I keep—yaas."

"Do ye now?" quoth Bessie, whose tongue was itching to mimic his affected Yankee drawl. "Troth, that's great—and sure you're a great man, Mr. Burke."

"Yaas—out there you'll find my wagons and my men in the streets, and my firm is pretty well known by now, I reckon. I stand straight on my feet—yaas. I guess my income just now figures out to some few thousand dollars. I've just come across for a little holiday trip, ye know, Mrs.—a—Phillips—just to see the old mother, ye know, an' some old friends. My baggage, I guess, is coming from the station just now."

He pulled out his watch and rubbed his fat fingers lovingly round its gold case; then twisted his rings, pulled his cuffs down till the links flashed, and spread his hands over his knees. Words could not have said plainer: Look at me, Bessie Darling; look at me, and gnash your teeth.

Bessie folded her arms and sat firmly before him. Ah! ye big, fat *bodach*, ye, she thought—this is what you've come for! Trying to

make little of me and show me what I did for myself. Thank the Lord!
I found a better man than ye. Sure I always doubted ye. Maybe if ye
went an' gave some o' your money to your ould mother over there it
wouldn't hurt her. Ye selfish, thick-headed ould bull! Sure it's
throwing good words away to talk to ye. But you're not going to sit
there and lord it over me— no, not if I know it.

"Yis," she said in her fluent, good-humored way, I heard talk ye
were doin' well, Mr. Burke—not that it mattered to *me;* but sure one
can't help people talkin'. Och, now, it's little time one has for talk.
What wi' *all* the pigs we have, an *all* the cattle, an' the ducks, an'
geese; an' makin' the butter—now one's little time to clack about any
one's affairs, much less strangers'. Th' other day, over rides Lord
Louth an' sits down there just where you're sittin', Mr. Burke, an' says
he: 'Faith, Mrs. Phillips, you're a lucky woman, so y' are, with the fine
man you've got,' says he, 'an' the industrious. You've the best farm,
Mrs. Phillips,' says he, 'an' the best stocked farm in the whole
property.' Ah! troth he made me blush, so he did; an' it was truth he
said, so it was. Ay! Ivery day on me two knees I thank God for all His
mercies."

"Yaas," said Tommy; "yaas."

"Ay! Lord Louth's the pleasantest gentleman," Bessie rattled on.
"Sure, he often comes to see us. Ay! a rale gentleman he is—a *rale*
gentleman. He comes in jist dressed like one av ourselves—not a ring
on him or a chain; an' he sits as 'umble there before us, Mr. Burke, as
one's own brother. Ay! an' he'll take tay from me—Mr. Burke, och!
what ails me? Sure, I must be dreamin'! Wid ye take a cup o' tay from
me? Sure, I'll make it in no time—now do! I've the finest butter an'
crame—the best in Irelan'. An' I'll whip ye up a bit o' flim cake in no
time – och, do!"

"Oh, no," said Tommy; "I must be goin'. I promised mother to be
back in an hour."

He fumbled with his hat, coughed, and prepared to rise.

"Ah, wait an' see Francy—ah, do!' pleaded Bessie. "Now he'll be
vexed if he doesn't see ye. He'll want to show ye the land, an' the
cattle, an' iverything. Well, you'll come again—now won't ye? Sure,
one likes to see ould friends. Whisht! here's the childer home from
school." She rapped at the window and brought two boys and a girl

through the garden to the front door. "Come in, childer," said she, "an'
see who's here—a whole live gentleman all the way from America.
Now, aren't they fine childer, Mr. Burke? Look at the limbs on them,
and them *that* healthy! Ay, indeed! An' sure the master spakes right
well o' their doin's at school. Sam here's in the third class already, an'
Bob there's out o' the first book." She ran her fingers through her little
daughter's flaxen hair, and stooped and kissed her rosy cheeks. "Bell
here's the darlin' child—ivery one likes her, don't they, Bell? Whisht!
me child, sure the fine gentleman won't hurt ye—he's only Mr. Burke
from America—ye know his mammy, don't ye, that lives in the wee
house over the bog?"

"Iss," answered Bell; "dirty ould Mother Burke."

Bessie put her hand tenderly over the child's mouth; then looked
straight at Tommy.

"Ye mus'n't mind childer, Mr. Burke," said she. "Ye know they pick
up all kinds o' talk at school. But they're the powerful blessin', so they
are—och, sure I wouldn't live without them!—What's that Sam?
Spake out, me son."

"I say, mother," said Sam in an awed whisper, "what makes him
wear his Sunday clothes on a weekday?"

"Ay, an' mother," chimed in Bob, "look at the big stumuck av—"

"Whisht," cried Bessie; "whisht! Where's your manners? I'm fair
'shamed o' ye both, so I am!"

Somehow Tommy felt uncomfortable; he rose quickly, and said he
must be going.

"Well, if you're goin', Mr. Burke," said Bessie, as she put out her
hand, "I suppose I mus'n't keep ye. Thank ye all the same, for comin'
to see me—sure it isn't every one'd come to see an' ould friend first
day home from foreign parts. But you'll come again soon an' see
Francy? He'll be powerful glad to know all about that gran' house o'
yours over the water—he cares to know more about that kind o' thing
than I do. Sure, what 'd the likes o' me know about such grandeur?
Goodbye, Mr. Burke."

His Magnificence went down the garden somewhat crestfallen;
somehow he felt that his visit had not been a success.

He opened the gate, and whilst it was on the swing the voice of
Sam the irrepressible came clear from behind.

"Mother," said Sam, "what in glory does the lad wear at the end o' that big brass chain?"

His Magnificence gave the gate a vicious pull and turned away in wrath.

But Bessie pulled the children into the hall, shut the door, put her hands on her hips, leant back against the wall, and laughed till the tears came.

Bob Pentland
William Carleton

THAT THE IRISH are a ready-witted people, is a fact to the truth of which testimony has been amply borne both by their friends and enemies. Many causes might be brought forward to account for this questionable gift, if it were our intention to be philosophical; but as the matter has been so generally conceded, it would be but a waste of logic to prove to the world that which the world cares not about, beyond the mere fact that it is so. On this or any other topic one illustration is worth twenty arguments, and, accordingly, instead of broaching a theory we shall relate a story.

Behind the hill or rather mountain of Altnaveenan lies one of those deep and almost precipitous valleys, on which the practiced eye of an illicit distiller would dwell with delight, as a topography not likely to be invaded by the unhallowed feet of the gauger [a revenue officer] and his red-coats. In point of fact, the spot we speak of was from its peculiarly isolated position nearly invisible, unless to such as came very close to it. Being so completely hemmed in and concealed by the round and angular projections of the mountain hills, you could never dream of its existence at all, until you came upon the very verge of the little precipitous gorge which led into it. This advantage of position was not, however, its only one. It is true, indeed, that the moment you had entered it, all possibility of its being applied to the purposes of distillation at once vanished, and you consequently could not help exclaiming, "what a pity that so safe and beautiful a nook should not have a single spot on which to erect a still-house, or rather on which to raise a sufficient stream of water to the elevation necessary for the process of distilling." If a gauger actually came to the little chasm, and cast his scrutinizing eye over it, he would immediately perceive that the erection of a private still in such a place was a piece of folly not generally to be found in the plans of those who have recourse to such practices.

This absence, however, of the requisite conveniences was only apparent, not real. To the right, about one hundred yards above the entrance to it, ran a ledge of rocks, some fifty feet high, or so. Along the lower brows, near the ground, grew thick matted masses of long heath, which covered the entrance to a cave about as large and as high as an ordinary farmhouse. Through a series of small fissures in the rocks which formed its roof, descended a stream of clear soft water, precisely in body and volume such as was actually required by the distiller; but, unless by lifting up this mass of heath, no human being could for a moment imagine that there existed any such grotto, or so unexpected and easy an entrance to it. Here there was a private still-house made by the hand of nature herself, such as no art or ingenuity of man could equal.

Now it so happened that about the period we write of, there lived in our parish two individuals so antithetical to each other in their pursuits of life, that we question whether throughout all the instinctive antipathies of nature we could find any two animals more destructive of each other than the two we mean—to wit, Bob Pentland, the gauger, and little George Steen, the illicit distiller. Pentland was an old, staunch, well-trained fellow, of about fifty years or more, steady and sure, and with all the characteristic points of the high-bred gauger about him. He was a tallish man, thin but lathy, with a hooked nose that could scent the tread of a distiller with the keenness of a slew-hound; his dark eye was deep-set, circumspect, and roguish in its expression, and his shaggy brow seemed always to be engaged in calculating whereabouts his inveterate foe, little George Steen, that eternally blinked him when almost in his very fangs, might then be distilling. To be brief, Pentland was proverbial for his sagacity and adroitness in detecting distillers, and little George was equally proverbial for having always baffled him, and that, too, sometimes under circumstances where escape seemed hopeless.

The incidents which we are about to detail occurred at that period of time when the collective wisdom of our legislators thought it advisable to impose a fine upon the whole townland in which the Still, Head, and Worm, might be found; thus opening a door for knavery and fraud, and, as it proved in most cases, rendering the innocent as liable to suffer for an offence they never contemplated as the guilty who planned and perpetrated it. The consequence of such a law was, that still-houses were always certain to be erected either at the very verge of the neighboring districts, or as near them as the circumstances of convenience and situation would permit. The moment of course that the hue-and-cry of the gauger and his myrmidons was heard upon the wind, the whole apparatus was immediately heaved over the *mering* to the next townland, from which the fine imposed by parliament was necessarily raised, whilst the crafty and offending district actually escaped. The state of society generated by such a blundering and barbarous statute as this, was dreadful. In the course of a short time, reprisals, law-suits, battles, murders, and massacres multiplied to such an extent throughout the whole country, that the sapient senators who occasioned such commotion were compelled to repeal their own act as soon as they found how it worked. Necessity, together with being the mother of invention, is also the cause of many an accidental discovery. Pentland had been so frequently defeated by little George, that he vowed never to rest until he had secured him; and George on the other hand frequently told him—for they were otherwise on the best terms— that he defied him, or as he himself more quaintly expressed it, "that he defied the devil, the world, and Bob Pentland." The latter, however, was a very sore thorn in his side, and drove him from place to place, and from one haunt to another, until he began to despair of being able any longer to outwit him, or to find within the parish any spot at all suitable to distillation with which Pentland was not acquainted. In this state stood matters between them, when George fortunately discovered at the hip of Altnaveenan hill the natural grotto we have just sketched so briefly. Now, George was a man, as we have already hinted, of great fertility of resources; but there existed in the same parish another distiller who outstripped him in that far-sighted cunning which is so necessary in misleading or circumventing such a sharp-scented old hound as Pentland. This was little Mickey M'Quade, a short-necked squat little fellow with bow legs, who might be said rather to creep in his motion than to walk. George and Mickey were intimate friends, independently of their joint antipathy against the gauger, and, truth to tell, much of the mortification and many of the defects which Pentland experienced at George's hands, were *sub rosa,* to be attributed to Mickey. George was a distiller from none of the motives which generally actuate others of that class. He was in truth an analytic philosopher—a natural chemist never out of some new experiment— and we have reason to think might have been the Kane, or Faraday, or

Dalton, of his day, had he only received a scientific education. Not so honest Mickey, who never troubled his head about an experiment, but only thought of making a good running, and defeating the gauger. The first thing of course that George did, was to consult Mickey, and both accordingly took a walk up to the scene of their future operations. On examining it, and fully perceiving its advantages, it might well be said that the look of exultation and triumph which passed between them was not unworthy of their respective characters.

"This will do," said George. "Eh—don't you think we'll put our finger in Pentland's eye yet!" Mickey spat sagaciously over his beard, and after a second glance gave one grave grin which spoke volumes. "It'll do," said he; "but there's one point to be got over that maybe you didn't think of; an' you know that half a blink, half a point, is enough for Pentland."

"What is it?"

"What do you intend to do with the smoke when the fire's lit?" There'll be no keepin' *that* down. Let Pentland see but as much smoke risin' as would come out of an ould woman's dudeen, an' he'd have us."

George started, and it was clear by the vexation and disappointment which were visible on his brow that unless this untoward circumstance could be managed, their whole plan was deranged, and the cave of no value.

"What's to be done?" he inquired of his cooler companion. "If we can't get over this, we may bid goodbye to it."

"Never mind," said Mickey; "I'll manage it, and *do* Pentland still."

"Ay, but how?"

"It's no matter. Let us not lose a minute in settin' to work. Lave the other thing to me; an' if I don't account for the smoke without discoverin' the entrance to the still, I'll give you lave to crop the ears off my head."

George knew the cool but steady self-confidence for which Mickey was remarkable, and accordingly without any further interrogatory, they both proceeded to follow up their plan of operations.

In those times when distillation might be truly considered as almost universal, it was customary for farmers to build their out-houses with secret chambers and other requisite partitions necessary for carrying it on. Several of them had private stores built between false walls, the entrance to which was only known to a few, and many of them had what were called *Malt-steeps* sunk in hidden recesses and hollow gables, for the purpose of steeping the barley, and afterwards of turning and airing it, until it was sufficiently hard to be kiln-dried and ground. From the mill it was usually conveyed to the still-house upon what were termed *Slipes*, a kind of car that was made without wheels, in order the more easily to pass through morasses and bogs which no wheeled vehicle could encounter.

In the course of a month or so, George and Mickey, aided by their friends, had all the apparatus of keeve, hogshead, &c., together with Still, Head, and Worm, set up and in full work.

"And now, Mickey," inquired his companion, "how will you manage about the smoke? for you know that the two worst informers against a private distiller, barrin' a *stag*, is a smoke by day, an' a fire by night."

"I know that," replied Mickey; "an' a rousin' smoke we'll have, for fraid a little puff wouldn't do us. Come, now, an' I'll show you."

They both ascended to the top, where Mickey had closed all the open fissures of the roof with the exception of that which was directly over the fire of the still. This was at best not more than six inches in breadth, and about twelve long. Over it he placed a piece of strong plate-iron perforated with holes, and on this he had a fire of turf, beside which sat a little boy who acted as a vidette. The thing was simple but effective. Clamps of turf were at every side of them, and the boy was instructed, if the gauger, whom he well knew, ever appeared, to heap on fresh fuel, so as to increase the smoke in such a manner as to induce him to suppose that *all* he saw of it proceeded merely from the fire before him. In fact, the smoke from the cave below was so completely identified with and lost in that which was emitted from the fire above, that no human being could penetrate the mystery, if not made previously acquainted with it. The writer of this saw it during the hottest process of distillation, and failed to make the discovery, although told that the still-house was within a circle of three hundred yards, the point he stood on being considered the center. On more than one occasion has he absconded from home, and spent a whole night in the place, seized with that indescribable fascination which such a

scene holds forth to youngsters, as well as from his irrepressible anxiety to hear the old stories and legends with the recital of which they generally pass the night.

In this way, well provided against the gauger—indeed much better than our readers are yet aware of, as they shall understand by and by— did George, Mickey, and their friends, proceed for the greater part of a winter without a single visit from Pentland. Several successful runnings had come off, which had of course turned out highly profitable, and they were just now preparing to commence their last, not only for the season, but the last they should ever work together, as George was making preparations to go early in the spring to America. Even this running was going on to their satisfaction, and the singlings had been thrown again into the still, from the worm of which projected the strong medicinal *first-shot* as the doubling commenced—this last term meaning the spirit in its pure and finished state. On this occasion the two worthies were more than ordinarily anxious, and certainly doubled their usual precautions against a surprise, for they knew that Pentland's visits resembled the pounces of a hawk or the springs of a tiger more than anything else to which they could compare them. In this they were not disappointed. When the doubling was about half finished he made his appearance, attended by a strong party of reluctant soldiers—for indeed it is due to the military to state that they never took delight in harassing the country people at the command of a key-hunter, as they generally nicknamed the gauger. It had been arranged that the vidette at the iron plate should whistle a particular tune the moment that the gauger or a red-coat, or in fact any person whom he did not know, should appear. Accordingly, about eight o'clock in the morning they heard the little fellow in his highest key whistling up that well-known and very significant old Irish air called "Go to the devil an' shake yourself"—which in this case was applied to the gauger in anything but an allegorical sense.

"Be the pins," which was George's usual oath, "be the pins, Mickey, it's over with us—Pentland's here, for there's the sign."

Mickey paused for a moment and listened very gravely, then squirting out a tobacco spittle, "Take it easy," said he; "I have half a dozen fires about the hills, any one as like this as your right hand is to your left. I didn't spare trouble, for I knew that if we'd get over *this* day, we'd be out of his power."

"Well, my good lad," said Pentland, addressing the vidette, "what's this fire for?"

"What is it for, is it?"

"Yes; if you don't let me know instantly, I'll blow your brains out, and get you hanged and transported afterwards."

This he said with a thundering voice, cocking a large horse pistol at the same time.

"Why, sir," said the boy, "it's watchin' a still I am: but be the hole o' my coat if you tell upon me, it's broilin' upon these coals I'll be soon."

"Where is the still, then? An' the still-house, where is it?"

"Oh, begorra, as to where the still or still-house is, they wouldn't tell *me* that."

"Why, sirra, didn't you say this moment you were watching a still?"

"I meant, sir," replied the lad, with a face that spoke of pure idiocy, "that it was the gauger I was watchin', an' I was to whistle upon my fingers to let the boy at that fire on the hill there above know he was comin'."

"Who told you to do so?"

"Little George, Sir, an' Mickey M'Quade."

"Ay, ay, right enough there, my lad—two of the most notorious schemers unhanged as they are both. But now, like a good boy, tell me the truth, an' I'll give you the price of a pair of shoes. Do you know where the still or still-house is? Because if you do, an' won't tell me, here are the soldiers at hand to make a prisoner of you; an' if they do, all the world can't prevent you from being hanged, drawn, and quartered."

"Oh, bad cess may seize the morsel o' me knows that; but if you'll give me the money, sir, I'll tell you who can bring you to it, for he tould me yestherday mornin' that he knew, an' offered to bring me there last night, if I'd steal him a bottle that my mother keeps the holy water in at home, tal he'd put whiskey in it."

"Well, my lad, who is this boy?"

"Do you know 'Harry Neil, or Mankind,'* sir?"

---

* *This was a nickname given to Harry, who was a cooper, and made the necessary vessels for distillers.*

"I do, my good boy."

"Well, it's a son of his, Sir; an' look, Sir: do you see the smoke farthest up to the right, Sir?"

"To the right? Yes."

"Well, 'tis there, Sir, that Darby Neil is watchin'; and he *says* he knows."

"How long have you been watching here?"

"This is only the third day, Sir, for *me;* but the rest, them boys above, has been here a good while."

"Have you seen nobody stirring about the hills since you came?"

"Only once, Sir, yestherday, I seen two men, havin' an empty sack or two, runnin' across the hill there above."

At this moment the military came up, for he had himself ran forward in advance of them, and he repeated the substance of his conversation with our friend the vidette. Upon examining the stolidity of his countenance, in which there certainly was a woeful deficiency of meaning, they agreed among themselves that his appearance justified the truth of the story which he told the gauger, and upon being further interrogated, they were confirmed that none but a stupid lout like himself would entrust to his keeping any secret worth knowing. They now separated themselves into as many detached parties as there were fires burning on the hills about them, the gauger himself resolving to make for that which Darby Neil had in his keeping, for he could not help thinking that the vidette's story was too natural to be false. They were just in the act of separating themselves to pursue their different routes, when the lad said,

"Look, Sir! look, Sir! bad scran be from me but there's a still any way. Sure I often seen a still: that's just like the one that Philip Hogan the tinker mended in George Steen's barn."

"Hollo, boys," exclaimed Pentland, "stoop! stoop! they are coming this way, and don't see us: no, hang them, no! they have discovered us now, and are off towards Mossfield. By Jove this will be a bitter trick if they succeed; confound them, they are bent for Ballagh, which is my own property; and may I be hanged but if we do not intercept them it is I myself who will have to pay the fine."

The pursuit instantly commenced with a speed and vigor equal to the ingenuity of this singular act of retaliation on the gauger. Pentland himself being long-winded from much practice in this way, and being further stimulated by the prospective loss which he dreaded, made as beautiful a run of it as any man of his years could do. It was all in vain, however. He merely got far enough to see the Still, Head, and Worm, heaved across the march ditch into his own property, and to reflect after seeing it that he was certain to have the double consolation of being made a standing joke of for life, and of paying heavily for the jest out of his own pocket. In the meantime, he was bound of course to seize the still, and report the caption; and as he himself farmed the townland in question, the fine was levied to the last shilling, upon the very natural principle that if he had been sufficiently active and vigilant, no man would have attempted to set up a still so convenient to his own residence and property.

This manoeuvre of keeping in reserve an old or second set of apparatus, for the purpose of acting the lapwing and misleading the gauger, was afterwards often practiced with success; but the first discoverer of it was undoubtedly Mickey M'Quade, although the honor of the discovery was attributed to his friend George Steen. The matter, however, did not actually end here, for in a few days afterwards some malicious wag—in other words, George himself—had correct information sent to Pentland touching the locality of the cavern and the secret of its entrance. On this occasion the latter brought a larger military party than usual along with him, but it was only to make him feel that he stood in a position, if possible, still more ridiculous than the first. He found indeed the marks of recent distillation in the place, but nothing else. Every vessel and implement connected with the process had been removed, with the exception of one bottle of whiskey, to which was attached by a bit of twine the following friendly note:—

"MR. PENTLAND, SIR—Take this bottle home and drink your own health. You can't do less. It was distilled *under your nose,* the first day you came to look for us, and bottled for you while you were speaking to the little boy that made a hare of you. Being distilled then under your nose, let it be drunk in the same place, and don't forget while doing so to drink the health of—G.S."

The incident went abroad like wildfire, and was known everywhere. Indeed for a long time it was the standing topic of the parish; and so sharply was it felt by Pentland that he could never keep his temper if asked, "Mr. Pentland, when did you see little George Steen?"—a question to which he was never known to give a civil reply.

The Gray Lake
Seumas O'Kelly

"I CAN SEE every color in the water except gray," said the lady who was something of a sceptic.

"That," said the humorist, tilting back his straw hat, "is the very reason they call it the Gray Lake. The world bristles with misnomers."

"Which explains," said the lady sceptic, "why they call Eamonn a *seannachie*."

"Hi!" called out the humorist. "Do you hear that, Eamonn?"

"*Cad tá ort?*" asked Eamonn. He had been leaning out over the prow of the boat, looking vaguely into the water, and now turned round. Eamonn was always asking people, "*Cad tá ort?*" and before they had time to answer he was saying, or thinking, something else.

"Why do they call this the Gray Lake?" asked the lady sceptic. "It never looked really gray, did it?"

"Of course it did," said Eamonn. "The first man who ever saw it beheld it in the gray light of dawn, and so he called it *Baile Loch Riabhach*, the Town of the Gray Lough."

"When might that be?" asked the lady sceptic drily.

"The morning after the town was drowned," said Eamonn.

"What town?"

"The town we are now rowing over."

"Good heavens! Is there a town beneath us?"

"*Seadh,*" said Eamonn. "Just now I was trying if I could see anything of the ruins at the bottom of the lake."

"And you did, of course."

"I think so."

"What did you see?"

"Confusion and the vague, glimmering gable of a house or two. Then the oars splashed and the water became dense."

"But tell us how the town came to be at the bottom of the lake," said the man who rowed, shipping his oars. The boat rocked in the quick wash of the waves. The water was warming in vivid colors under the glow of the sunset. Eamonn leaned back in his seat at the prow of the boat. His eyes wandered away over the water to the slope of

107

meadows, the rise of hills.

"*Anois, Eamonn,*" said the lady sceptic, still a little drily. "The story!"

Long and long ago, said Eamonn, there was a sleepy old town lying snug in the dip of a valley. It was famous for seven of the purest springs of water which ever sparkled in the earth. They called it the Seven Sisters. Round the springs they built an immense and costly well. Over the well was a great leaden lid of extraordinary weight, and by a certain mechanical device this lid was closed on the well every evening at sundown. The springs became abnormally active between sundown and sunrise, so that there was always a danger that they might flood the valley and destroy the people. As security against this the citizens had built the great well with its monster lid, and each evening the lid was locked over the well by means of a secret lock and a secret key.

The most famous person in the town of the Seven Sisters was the Keeper of the Key. He was a man of dignified bearing, important airs, wearing white silk knee-breeches, a green swallow-tail coat, and a cocked hat. On the sleeve of his coat was embroidered in gold the image of a key and seven sprays of water. He had great privileges and authority, and could condemn or reprieve any sort of criminal except, of course, a sheep stealer. He lived in a mansion beside the town, and this mansion was almost as famous as the seven famous springs. People traveled from far places to see it. A flight of green marble steps led to a broad door of oak. On the broad oaken door he had fashioned one of the most remarkable knockers and the most beautiful door knob that were known to Europe. Both were of beaten gold. The knocker was wrought in the shape of a key. The door knob was a group of seven water nymphs. A sensation was created which agitated all Ireland when this work of art was completed by five of the foremost goldsmiths in the land. The Keeper of the Key of the Seven Sisters issued a Proclamation declaring that there was a flaw in the rounding of one of the ankles of the group of seven water nymphs. He had the five goldsmiths suddenly arrested and put on their trial. "The Gael," said the Keeper of the Key, "must be pure-blooded in his art. I am of the Clann Gael. I shall not allow any half-artist to come to my door, there work under false pretense and go unpunished." The goldsmiths protested that their work was the work of artists and flawless as the design. Not another word would they be allowed to speak. Bards and artists, scholars and men skilled in controversy, flocked from all parts to see the door knob. A terrible controversy ensued. Sides were taken, some for, others against, the ankle of the water nymph. They came to be known as the Ankleites and the anti-Ankleites. And in that tremendous controversy the Keeper of the Key proved the masterly manner of man he was. He had the five goldsmiths convicted for failure as supreme artists, and they were sentenced to banishment from the country. On their way from the shore to the ship that was to bear them away, their curragh sprang a sudden leak, and they were all drowned. That was the melancholy end of the five chief goldsmiths of Eirinn.

Every morning at daybreak trumpets were blown outside the mansion of the Keeper of the Key. The gates of a courtyard swung open and out marched an armed guard, men in saffron kilts, bearing spears and swords. They formed up before the flight of marble steps. A second fanfare of the trumpets, and back swung the great oaken door, disclosing the Keeper of the Key in his bright silks and cocked hat. Out he would come on the doorstep, no attendants by him, and pulling to the great door by the famous knob he would descend the marble steps, the guard would take up position, and, thus escorted, he would cross the drawbridge of the moat and enter the town of the Seven Sisters, marching through the streets to the great wall. People would have gathered there even at that early hour, women bearing vessels to secure their supply of the water, which, it was said, had an especial virtue when taken at the break of day. No mortal was allowed nearer than fifty yards to the well while the Keeper proceeded to unlock the lid. His guard would stand about, and with a haughty air he would approach the well solus. The people would see him make some movements, and back would slide the enormous lid. A blow on the trumpets proclaimed that the well was open, and the people would approach it, laughing and chattering, and the Keeper of the Key would march back to his mansion in the same military order, ascend the steps, push open the great door, and the routine of daily life would ensue. For the closing of the well at sundown a similar ceremony was observed. The only additional incident was the marching of a crier through the streets, beating great wooden clappers, and standing at each street corner calling out in a loud voice: "Hear ye people that the lock is on the Seven Sisters. All's well!"

In those days there was a saying among the people which was in common usage all over Ireland. When a man became possessed of any article or property to which he had a doubtful title his neighbors said, with a significant wag of the head, "He got it where the Keeper gets the Key." This saying arose out of a mysterious thing in the life of the Keeper of the Key. Nobody ever saw the secret key. It was not in his hands when he came forth from the mansion morning and evening to fulfil his great office. He did not carry it in his pockets, for the simple reason that he had no pockets. He kept no safe nor secret panel nor any private drawer in his mansion that the most observant among his retainers would espy. Yet that there was a secret key, and that it was inserted in a lock, anybody could see for himself, even at a distance of fifty yards, twice a day at the well. It was as if at that moment the key came into his hand out of the air and again vanished into air when the proper business was over. Indeed, there were people of even those remote and enlightened days who attributed some wizardry to the Keeper of the Key. It added to the awe in which he was held and to the sense of security which the proceedings of his whole life inspired in his fellow-citizens. Nevertheless had the Keeper of the Key his enemies. A man of distinction and power can no more tread the paths of his ambitions without stirring up rivalries and hostilities than can the winds howl across the earth and leave the dust on the roads undisturbed. The man who assumes power will always, sooner or later, have his power to hold put to the test. So it was with the Keeper of the Key. There were people who nursed the ambition of laying hands on the secret key. That secured, they would be lords of the town of the Seven Sisters. The reign of the great Keeper would be over. His instinct told him that these dangers were always about. He was on the alert. He had discovered treachery even within the moat of his own keep. His servants and guards had been tampered with. But all the attempts upon his key and his power had been in vain. He kept to the grand unbroken simplicity of his masterly routine. He had crushed his enemies whenever they had arisen. "One who has survived the passions of Ireland's poets," he would say—for the poets had all been Ankleites— "is not likely to bow the knee before sniveling little thieves." A deputation which had come to him proposing that the well should be managed by a constitutional committee of the citizens was flogged by the guards across the drawbridge. The leader of this deputation was a deformed tailor, who soon after planned an audacious attack on the mansion of the Keeper of the Key. The Keeper, his guards, servants and retainers were all one night secretly drugged and for several hours of the night lay unconscious in the mansion. Into it swarmed the little tailor and his constitutional committee; they pulled the whole interior to pieces in search of the key. The very pillows under the head of the Keeper had been stabbed and ransacked. It was nearing daybreak when the Keeper awoke, groggy from the effects of the narcotic. The guard was roused. The whole place was in confusion. The robbers had fled, leaving the great golden knocker on the door hanging from its position; they were removing it when surprised. The nymphs were untouched. The voice of the Keeper of the Key was deliberate, authoritative, commanding, amid the confusion. The legs of the guards quaked beneath them, their heads swam, and they said to each other, "Now surely is the key gone!" But their master hurried them to their morning duty, and they escorted him to the well a little beyond daybreak, and, lo, at the psychological moment, there was the key and back rolled the lid from the precious well. "Surely," they said, "this man is blessed, for the key comes to him as a gift from Heaven. The robbers of the earth are powerless against him." When the citizens of the Seven Sisters heard of what had taken place in the evil hours of the night they poured across the drawbridge from the town and acclaimed the Keeper of the Key before his mansion. He came out on the watch tower, his daughter by his side, and with dignified mien acknowledged the acclamations of the citizens. And before he put the lid on the well that night the deformed tailor and his pards were all dragged through the streets of the Seven Sisters and cast into prison.

Never was the popularity of the Keeper at so high a level as after this episode. They would have declared him the most perfect as the most powerful of men were it not for one little spot on the bright sun of his fame. They did not like his domestic habits. The daughter who stood by his side on the watch tower was a young girl of charm, a fair,

frail maiden, a slender lily under the towering shadow of her dark
father. The citizens did not, perhaps, understand his instincts of
paternity; and, indeed, if they understood them they would not have
given them the sanction of their approval. The people only saw that the
young girl, his only child, was condemned to what they called a life of
virtual imprisonment in the mansion. She was a warm-blooded young
creature, and like all warm-blooded creatures, inclined to gaiety of
spirits, to impulsive friendships, to a joyous and engaging frankness.
These traits, the people saw, the father disapproved of and checked,
and the young girl was regarded with great pity. "Ah," they would say,
"he is a wonderful Keeper of the Key, but, alas, how harsh a father!"
He would not allow the girl any individual freedom; she was under
eternal escort when abroad; she was denied the society of those of her
years; she was a flower whose fragrance it was not the privilege of the
people to enjoy. It may be that the people, in murmuring against all
this, did not make sufficient allowance for the circumstances of the life
of the Keeper of the Key. He was alone, he stood apart from all men.
His only passion in life had been the strict guardianship of a trust. In
these circumstances his affections for his only child were direct and
crude and, too, maybe a little unconsciously harsh. His love for his
child was the love of the oyster for its pearl. The people saw nothing
but the rough, tight shells which closed about the treasure in the
mansion of the Keeper of the Key. More than one considerable wooer
had approached that mansion, laying claim to the pearl which it held.
All were met with the same terrible dark scowl and sent about their
business. "You, Sir," the Keeper of the Key would say, "come to my
door, knock upon my knocker, lay hands upon my door knob—my
golden door knob—and ask for my daughter's hand! Sir, your audacity
is your only excuse. Let it also be your defense against my wrath.
Now, sir, a very good day!" And when the citizens heard that yet
another gallant wooer had come and been dismissed they would say,
"The poor child, the poor child, what a pity!"

The truth was that the daughter of the Keeper of the Key was not in
the least unhappy. She had a tremendous opinion of her father; she
lavished upon him all the warm affection of her young ardor. She
reigned like a young queen within the confines of her home. She was
about the gardens and the grounds all day, as joyous as a bird. Once or

twice her governess gave her some inkling as to the suitors who came
to the mansion requesting her hand, for that is an affair that cannot be
kept from the most jealously-guarded damsel. The governess had a
sense of humor and entertained the girl with accounts of the manner of
lovers who, as she put it, washed up the marble steps of the mansion to
the oak door, like waves on a shore, and were sent back again into the
ocean of rejections. The young girl was much amused and secretly
flattered at these events. "Ah," she would say, in a little burst of
rapture, "how splendid is my father!" The pearl rejoices in the power
of the oyster to shut it away from the world.

Now (continued Eamonn), on the hilly slopes of the country called
Sunnach there was a shepherd boy, and people who saw that he was a
rare boy in looks and intelligence were filled with pity for his unhappy
lot. The bodach for whom he herded was a dour, ill-conditioned
fellow, full of curses and violent threats, but the boy was content in the
life of the hillsides, and troubled very little about the bodach's dour
looks. "Some day," he would say to himself laughingly, "I will
compose terrible verses about his black mouth." One day the shepherd
boy drove a little flock of the bodach's lively sheep to the fair in the
town of the Seven Sisters. As he passed the mansion of the Keeper of
the Key he cried out, "How up! how up! how up!" His voice was clear
and full, the notes as round and sweet as the voice of the cuckoo. The
daughter of the Keeper of the Key was seated by a window painting a
little picture when she heard the "How up!" of the shepherd's voice.
"What beautiful calls!" she exclaimed, and leaned out from the
window. At the same moment the shepherd boy looked up. He was
bare-headed and wore his plaids. His head was a shock of curly straw-
colored hair, his face eager, clear-cut, his eyes golden-brown and
bright as the eyes of a bird. He smiled and the damsel smiled. "How
up! how up! how up!" he sang out joyously to his flock as he moved
down to the fair. The damsel went back to her little picture and sat
there for some time staring at her palette and mixing the wrong colors.

That evening the Keeper of the Key, as was his custom, escorted his
daughter on his arm, servants before and behind them, through the
town of the Seven Sisters, viewing such sights of the fair as were
agreeable and doing a little shopping. The people, seeing the great
man coming, made way for him on the paths, and bowed and smiled to

him as he passed. He walked with great dignity, and his daughter's beauty made the bystanders say, "Happy will it be for the lucky man!" Among those they encountered was the shepherd boy, and he gazed upon the damsel with rapture in his young eyes. He followed them about the town at a respectful distance, and back to their mansion. The shepherd boy did not return to the hilly country called Sunnach that night, nor the next night, nor for many a long day and night. He remained in the town of the Seven Sisters, running on errants, driving carts, doing such odd jobs as came his way, and all because he wanted to gaze upon the daughter of the Keeper of the Key. In the evening he would go by the mansion singing out, "How up! how up! how up!" as if he were driving flocks past. And in the window he would see the wave of a white hand. He would go home, then, to his little back room in the lodging-house, and there stay up very late at night, writing, in the candle-light, verses to the damsel. One Song of the Shepherd Boy to his Lady has survived:

Fairwell to the sweet reed I tuned on the
hill,
My grief for the rough slopes of Sunnach
so still,
The wind in the fir tree and bleat of the
ewe
Are lost in the wild cry my heart makes for
you.
The brown floors I danced on, the sheds
where I lay,
Are gone from my mind like a wing in the
bay:
Dear lady, I'd herd the wild swans in the
skies
If they knew of lake water as blue as your
eyes!

Well, it was not very long, as you can imagine, until the Keeper of the Key observed the shepherd boy loitering about the mansion. When he heard him calling past the house to imaginary flocks, a scowl came upon his face. "Ah-ha!" he said, "another conspiracy! Last time it was a hunchback tailor. This time they come from the country. They signal by the cries of shepherds. Well, I shall do the driving for them!" There and then he had the shepherd boy apprehended, bound, and put in a cell. In due course he was accused and sentenced, like the famous goldsmiths, to banishment from Eirinn. When the daughter of the Keeper heard what had come to pass she was filled with grief. She appeared before her father for the first time with tears in her eyes and woe in her face. He was greatly moved, and seated the girl by his side. She knelt by his knee and confessed to the whole affair with the shepherd boy. The Keeper of the Key was a little relieved to learn that his suspicions of a fresh conspiracy were unfounded, but filled with indignation that such a person as a shepherd should not alone aspire to but win the heart of his daughter. "What have we come to," he said, "when a wild thing from the hills of Sunnach comes down and dares to lay his hand on the all but perfect water nymphs on the golden knob of my door! Justice shall be done. The order of banishment is set aside. Let this wild hare of the hills, this mountain rover, be taken and seven times publicly dipped in the well. I guarantee that will cool him! He shall then have until break of day to clear out of my town. Let him away back to the swine on the hills." The girl pleaded that the boy might be spared the frightful indignity of a public dipping in the well of the Seven Sisters, but her father was implacable. "Have I not spoken?" he said sternly, and the damsel was led away by her governess in tears.

The people flocked to the well as they might to a Feis to see the dipping of the shepherd boy. Cries of merriment arose among them when the boy, bound in strips of hide, was lowered by the servants of the Keeper of the Key into the mouth of the great well. It was a cold, dark, creepy place down in the shaft of the well, the walls reeking, covered with slimy green lichen, the waters roaring. The shepherd boy closed his eyes and gave himself up for lost. But the Seven Sisters of the well kept moving down as fast as the servants told out the rope, until at last they could not lower him any farther. The servants danced the rope up and down seven.times, and the people screamed and clapped their hands, crying out, "All those who write love verses come to a bad end!" But the poet was never yet born who had not a friend greater than all his enemies. At that moment the spirits of the Seven Sisters rose out of the water and spoke to the shepherd boy.

"Oh shepherd boy," they said, "the Keeper of the Key is also our enemy. We were created for something better than this narrow shaft. We cry out in bitter pain the long hours of the night."

"Why do you cry out in bitter pain?" asked the shepherd boy.

"Because," said the spirits of the Seven Sisters, "we want to leap out of this cold place to meet our lover, the moon. Every night he comes calling to us and we dare not respond. We are locked away under the heavy lid. We can never gather our full strength to burst our way to liberty. We dream of the pleasant valley. We want to get out into it, to make merry about the trees, to sport in the warm places, to lip the edge of the green meadows, to water pleasant gardens. We want to see the flowers, to flash in the sun, to dance under the spread of great branches, to make snug, secret places for the pike and the otter, to pile up the colored pebbles, and hear the water-hen splashing in the rushes. And above all, we want to meet our lover, the moon, to roll about in his beams, to reach for his kiss in the harvest nights. O shepherd boy, take us from our prison well!"

"O Seven Sisters," asked the shepherd boy, "how can I do this for you?"

"Secure the secret key," they said. "Open the lid while we are at our full strength in the night."

"Alas," said the shepherd boy, "that I cannot do. The Keeper has made of it a magic thing."

"We know his great secret," said the spirits of the Seven Sisters. "Swear to set us free and we shall tell you the secret of the key."

"And what reward shall I have?" asked the shepherd boy.

"You shall have the hand of the daughter of the Keeper of the Key, the Lady of your Songs," they said. "Take her back to the hills where you were so happy. We shall spare you when we are abroad."

"Then," said the shepherd boy, "I swear to release you."

"The Keeper of the Key," said the spirits of the Seven Sisters, "has a devil lurking behind the fine manners of his body. In secret he laughs at the people. He has the blood of the five goldsmiths on his hands. It was by his connivance the curragh sprang a leak, and that they were drowned. They were true artists, of the spirit of the Gael. But they alone knew his secret, and he made away with them before they could speak. His great controversy on the water nymphs was like a spell cast over the minds of the people to cover his crime."

"What a demon!" cried the shepherd boy.

"The key of the well," said the spirits of the Seven Sisters, "is concealed in the great golden knob of the oaken door, and upon that has concentrated the greatest public scrutiny which has ever beaten upon a door-knob in the story of the whole world. Such has been the craft of the Keeper of the Key! When he comes out in the morning and evening, and while drawing the door after him, he puts a finger on the third toe of the fourth water nymph. This he presses three times, quick as a pulse-beat, and, lo, a hidden spring is released and shoots the key into the loose sleeve of his coat. On returning he puts his hand on the golden knob, presses the second toe of the third water nymph, and the key slides back into its hidden cavity. This secret was alone known to the goldsmiths. They went to the bottom of the sea with it. In this way has the Keeper of the Key held his power and defied his enemies. When the scholars were making epigrams and the bards warming into great cadences on the art of the ankle of the water nymph, this Keeper of the Key would retire to his watch tower and roll about in secret merriment."

"What a fiend!" cried the shepherd boy.

"He had caused to be painted in his room a scroll surrounded by illuminated keys and nymphs and tumbling cascades, and bearing the words, 'Let us praise the art which conceals art; but let us love the art which conceals power.' "

"What a monster!" cried the shepherd boy.

"In this way," said the spirits of the Seven Sisters, "has he lived. In this way has he been able to keep us from our freedom, our lover. O shepherd boy—"

Before another word could be spoken the shepherd boy was drawn up on the rope. The water rose with him and lapped lightly over his person so that he might seem as if he had been plunged deeply into the well.

When he was drawn up to the side of the well the shepherd boy lay on the ground, his eyes closed, feigning great distress. The people again clapped their hands, and some cried out, "Now little water rat, make us a new verse!" But others murmured in pity, and an old peasant woman, in a Breedeen cloak, hobbled to his side and smoothed back his locks. At the touch of her soft hands the shepherd boy opened his eyes, and he saw it was the the daughter of the Keeper of the Key disguised. With the connivance of her governess, she had escaped from the mansion as an old peasant woman in a cloak. The shepherd boy secretly kissed her little palms and whispered, "I must come to you at midnight. As you value your life have the guards taken from the outer door only for two minutes. Make some pretext. I will give the shepherd's call and then you must act. Do not fail me."

Before more could be said the servants roughly bundled the old peasant woman aside, carried the shepherd boy to his lodgings, and there threw him on his bed. "Remember," they said, "that you remain within the walls of the town of the Seven Sisters after break of day at your peril."

At midnight the shepherd boy arose and approached the mansion of the Keeper of the Key. He could see the two grim guards, one each side of the oaken door. Standing some way off he gave the shepherd's call, making his voice sound like the hoot of an owl. In a little time he saw the guards move away from the door; they went to a side entrance in the courtyard, and presently he could hear them laughing, as if some entertainment was being provided for them; then measures were passed through the iron bars of the gate to them, and these they raised to their lips. At this the shepherd boy ran swiftly up the steps, approached the door, and pressed three times, quick as a pulse-beat, the third toe of the fourth water nymph, and immediately from a secret cavity of the knob a curious little golden key was shot forth. This the shepherd boy seized, flew down the steps, and scaled over the town wall. He ran to the great well and stooped over the lid. He could hear the Seven Sisters twisting and worming and striving beneath it, little cries of pain breaking from them. Overhead the moon was shining down on the well.

"O Seven Sisters," said the Shepherd boy, "I have come to give you to your lover."

He could hear a great cry of joy down in the well. He put the key in the lock, turned it, and immediately there was the gliding and slipping of one steel bar after another into an oil bath. The great lid slowly revolved, moving away from over the well. The Seven Sisters did the rest. They sprang with a peal of the most delirious laughter—laughter that was of the underground, the cavern, the deep secret places of the earth, laughter of elfs and hidden rivers—to the light of the moon. The shepherd boy could see seven distinct spiral issues of sparkling water and they took the shape of nymphs, more exquisite than anything he had ever seen even in his dreams. Something seemed to happen in the very heavens above; the moon reached down from the sky, swiftly and tenderly, and was so dazzling that the shepherd boy had to turn his face away. He knew that in the blue spaces of the firmament overhead the moon was embracing the Seven Sisters. Then he ran, ran like the wind, for already the water was shrieking down the streets of the town. As he went he could see lights begin to jump in dark windows and sleepy people in their night attire coming to peer out into the strange radiance outside.

As he reached the drawbridge he saw that the men had already lowered it, and there was a great rustling noise and squealing; and what he took to be a drift of thick dust driven by the wind was gushing over it, making from the town. A few more yards and he saw that it was not thick brown dust, but great squads of rats flying the place. The trumpets were all blowing loud blasts when he reached the mansion of the Keeper of the Key, the guards with their spears pressing out under the arch of the courtyard, and servants coming out the doors. The great oak door flew open and he saw the Keeper of the Key, a candle in his quaking hand. A great crying could now be heard coming up from the population of the town. The water was bursting upon the doors of the houses as if they were cardboard.

"O Keeper of the Key," cried the shepherd boy, "the Seven Sisters are abroad. I am obeying your command and returning to the swine on the hills. The despised Sunnach will be in the dreams of many to-night!"

The candle fell from the hand of the Keeper of the Key, and he could be seen in the moonlight groping for the door-knob, his hand on the figures of the group of water nymphs. In a moment he gave a low moan and, his head hanging over his breast, he staggered down the marble steps. "Alas," cried the guards, "now is the great man broken!" He made for the drawbridge crying out, "The lid, the lid. Slide it back over the well!" The guards and servants pressed after him, but not one of them ever got into the town again. Across the bridge was now pouring a wild rush of human panic. Carriages, carts, cars, horsemen, mules, donkeys, were flying from the Seven Sisters laden with men and women and whole families. Crowds pressed forward on foot. Animals, dogs, cats, pigs, sheep, cows, came pell-mell with them. Drivers stood in their seats flaying their horses as if driven by madness. The animals rolled their eyes, snorted steam from their nostrils, strained forward with desperate zeal. Once or twice the struggling mass jammed, and men fought each other like beasts. The cries of people being trampled to death broke out in harrowing protest. For a moment the shepherd boy saw the form of a priest rise up, bearing aloft the stark outline of a cross, and then he disappeared.

Over that night of terror was the unnatural brilliance of the swollen moon. All this the shepherd boy saw in a few eternal moments. Then he cried out, "How up! how up! how up!" and immediately the damsel tripped down the broad staircase of the mansion, dressed in white robes, her hair loose about her shoulders. Never had she looked so frail and beautiful, the lily of the valley! The shepherd boy told her what had come to pass. She cried out for her father. "I am the daughter of the Keeper of the Key," she said, "I shall stand by his side at the well in this great hour."

"I am now the master of the town of the Seven Sisters," said the shepherd boy, "I am the Keeper of the Key." And he held up the secret key.

The damsel, seeing this, and catching sight of what was taking place at the drawbridge, fell back in a swoon on the carpet of the hall. The shepherd boy raised her in his arms and fled for the hills. Along the road was the wild stampede of the people, all straining for the hills, pouring in a mad rush from the valley and the town. Behind them were the still madder, swifter, more terrible waters, coming in sudden thuds, in furious drives, eddying and sculping and rearing in an orgy of remorseless and heartrending destruction. Down before that roaring avalanche went walls and trees and buildings. The shepherd boy saw men give up the struggle for escape, cowering by the roadside, and women, turning from the race to the hills, rushed back to meet the oncoming waters with arms outspread and insanity in their wild eyes.

Not a human creature escaped that night of wroth except the shepherd boy and the damsel he carried in his arms. Every time the waters reached his heels they reared up like great white horses and fell back, thus sparing him. Three times did he look back at happenings in the town of the Seven Sisters. The first time he looked back the water was up to the last windows of houses that were three storeys high. All the belongings of the householders were floating about, and people were sinking through the water, their lives going out as swiftly as twinkling bubbles. In an attic window he saw a young girl loosen her hair, she was singing a song, preparing to meet death as if she were making ready for a lover. A man at the top of a ladder was gulping whiskey from a bottle, and when the water sprang at his throat he went down with a mad defiant cry. A child ran out an open window, golden locks dancing about its pretty head, as if it were running into a garden. There was another little bubble in the moonlight . . . . The second time the shepherd boy looked back the swallows were flying from their nests under the eaves of the houses, for the water was now lapping them. An old woman was hobbling across a roof on crutches. Men were drawing their bodies out of the chimney-pots. A raft on which the Keeper's guard had put out slowly, like a live thing lazily yawning and turning over on its side, sent them all into the common doom. A man with a bag of gold clutched in his hand, stood dizzily on the high gable of a bank, then, with a scream, tottered and fell . . . . The third time the shepherd boy looked back nothing was to be seen above the face of the water except the pinnacle of the watch tower of the mansion, and standing upon it was the Keeper of the Key, his arms outspread, his face upturned to the moon, and the seven water nymphs leaping about him in a silver dance.

After that the shepherd boy drew up on the hills with the damsel. He was quite exhausted, and he noticed that the activity of the waters gradually calmed down as daybreak approached, like things spent after a night of wild passion. When at last the day quivered into life on the eastern sky, he called the damsel to his side, and standing there together they looked out over the spread of water. The town of the Seven Sisters was no more.

"Look," cried the shepherd boy, "at Loch Riabhach!" And drawing back he cast out into the far water the secret key. There it still lies under a rock, somewhere in the lake over which our boat is now drifting. And the shepherd boy and the damsel there and then founded a new town beside the lake, and all who are of the old families of Baile Loch Riabhach, like myself, are their descendants. That, concluded Eamonn, is the story of the Gray Lake.

The Devil's Mill
Samuel Lover

BESIDE the river Liffey, stands the picturesque ruin of a mill, overshadowed by some noble trees that grow in great luxuriance at the water's edge. Here, one day, I was accosted by a silver-haired old man, that for some time had been observing me, and who, when I was about to leave the spot, approached me, and said, "I suppose it's afther takin' off the ould mill you'd be, Sir?"

I replied in the affirmative.

"Maybe your honor id let me get a sight iv it," said he.

"With pleasure," said I, as I untied the strings of my portfolio, and, drawing the sketch from amongst its companions, presented it to him. He considered it attentively for some time, and at length exclaimed, "Throth there it is, to the life—the broken roof and the wather coorse; aye, even to the very spot where the gudgeon of the wheel was wanst, let alone the big stone at the corner that was laid the first, by *himself*"; and he gave the last word with mysterious emphasis, and handed the drawing back to me with a "thankee, Sir," of most respectful acknowledgment.

"And who was 'himself,'" said I, "that laid that stone?" feigning ignorance, and desiring "to draw him out," as the phrase is.

"Oh, then, maybe it's what you'd be a stranger here," said he.

"Almost," said I.

"And did you never hear tell of L———'s mill," said he, "and how it was built?"

"Never," was my answer.

"Throth then I thought young and ould, rich and poor, knew that— far and near."

"I don't, for one," said I; "but perhaps," I added, bringing forth some little preparation for a lunch, that I had about me, and producing a small flask of whiskey—"perhaps you will be so good as to tell me, and take a slice of ham and drink my health," offering him a dram from my flask, and seating myself on the sod beside the river.

"Thank you kindly, Sir," says he; and so, after "warming his heart," as he said himself, he proceeded to give an account of the mill in question.

124

"You see, Sir, there was a man wonst, in times back, that owned a power o' land about here, but God keep uz, they say he didn't come by it honestly, but did a crooked turn whenever 't was to sarve himself—and sure he *sowld the pass*,* and what luck or grace could he have afther that?"

"How do you mean he sold the pass?" said I.

"Oh, sure your honor must have heerd how the pass was sowld, and he bethrayed his king and counthry."

"No, indeed," said I.

"Och, well," answered my old informant, with a shake of the head, which he meant, like Lord Burleigh in the *Critic*, to be very significant, "it's no matther now, and I don't care talkin' about it; and laste said is soonest mended—howsomever, he got a power of money for that same, and lands and what not; but the more he got, the more he craved, and there was no ind to his sthrivin' for goold evermore, and thirstin' for the lucre of gain.

"Well, at last, the story goes, the Divil, (God bless us,) kem to him and promised him hapes o' money, and all his heart could desire, and more too, if he'd sell his sowl in exchange."

"Surely he did not consent to such a dreadful bargain as that," said I.

"Oh no, Sir," said the old man, with a slight play of muscle about the corners of his mouth, which, but that the awfulness of the subject suppressed it, would have amounted to a bitter smile—"Oh no—he was too cunnin' for that, bad as he was—and he was bad enough, God knows—he had some regard for his poor sinful sowl, and he would not give himself up to the Divil, all out; but the villain, he thought he might make a bargain with the *ould chap*, and get all he wanted, and keep himself out of harm's way still: for he was mighty cute—and throth he was able for ould Nick any day.

"Well, the bargain was struck, and it was this-a-way: The Divil was to give him all the goold ever he'd ask for, and was to let him alone as long as he could; and the timpter promised him a long day, and said 'twould be a great while before he'd want him at all, at all; and whin that time kem, he was to keep his hands aff him, as long as the other

* *An allusion to a post of importance that was betrayed in some of the battles between William III. and James II.*

could give him some work he couldn't do.

"So, when the bargain was made, 'Now,' says the Colonel to the Divil, 'give me all the money I want.'

"'As much as you like,' says Ould Nick—'how much will you have?'

"'You must fill me that room,' says he, pointin' into a murtherin' big room, that he emptied out on purpose—'you must fill me that room,' says he, 'up to the very ceilin' with goolden guineas.'

"'And welkim,' says the Divil.

"With that, Sir, he began to shovel in the guineas into the room, like mad; and the Colonel towld him, that as soon as he was done, to come to him in his own parlor below, and that he would then go up and see if the Divil was as good as his word, and had filled his room with the goolden guineas. So the Colonel went down stairs, and the Ould Fellow worked away as busy as a nailer, shovellin' in the guineas by hundherds and thousands.

"Well, he worked away for an hour, and more, and at last he began to get tired; and he thought it *mighty odd* that the room wasn't fillin' fasther. Well, afther restin' for a while, he began agin, and he put his shouldher to the work in airnest; but still the room was no fuller, at all, at all.

"'Och! bad luck to me,' says the Divil, 'but the likes of this I never seen,' says he, 'far and near, up and down—the dickens a room I ever kem across afore,' says he, 'I couldn't cram, while a cook would be crammin' a turkey, till now; and here I am,' says he, 'losin' my whole day, and I with such a power o' work an my hands yit, and this room no fuller than if I began five minutes ago.

"By gor, while he was spaakin', he seen the hape o' guineas in the middle of the flure growin' *littler and littler* every minit; and at last, they wor disappearin', for all the world, like corn in the hopper of a mill.

"'Ho! ho!' says Ould Nick, 'is that the way wid you?' says he; and with that, he run over to the hape of goold, and, what would you think, but it was runnin' down through a big hole in the flure, that the Colonel made through the ceilin', in the room below; and that was the work he was at afther he left the Divil, though he purtended he was only waitin' for him in his parlor, and there, the Divil, when he looked

down through the hole in the flure, seen the Colonel, not content with
the two rooms full of guineas, but, with a big shovel, throwin' them
into a closet a one side of him, as fast as they fell down. So, puttin' his
head through the hole, he called down to the Colonel:—

"'Hillo! neighbor,' says he.

"The Colonel looked up, and grew as white as a sheet when he seen
he was found out, and the red eyes starin' down at him through the
hole.

"'Musha! bad luck to your impudence,' says Owld Nick: 'is it
sthrivin' to chate *me* you are,' says he, 'you villain?'

"'Oh! forgive me this wanst,' says the Colonel, 'and upon the honor
of a gintleman,' says he, 'I'll never—'

"'Whisht! whisht! you thievin' rogue,' says the Divil—'I'm not
angry with you, at all, at all, but only like you the betther, bekase
you're so cute—lave off slaving yourself there,' says he, 'you have got
goold enough for this time; and whenever you want more, you have
only to say the word, and it shall be yours at command.'

"So, with that, the Divil and he parted for that time; and myself
doesn't know whether they used to meet often afther, or not; but the
Colonel never wanted money, anyhow, but went on prosperous in the
world, and, as the saying is, if he tuk the dirt out o' the road, it id turn
to money wid him; and so, in coorse of time, he bought great estates,
and was a great man intirely—not a greater in Ireland, throth."

Fearing here a digression on landed interest, I interrupted him, to
ask, how he and the fiend settled their account at last.

"Oh, Sir, you'll hear that all in good time. Sure enough, it's terrible,
and wondherful it is, at the end, and mighty improvin'—glory be to
God."

"Is that what you say," said I, in surprise, "because a wicked and
deluded man lost his soul to the tempter?"

"Oh, the Lord forbid, your honor; but don't be impatient, and you'll
hear all. They say, at last, afther many years of prosperity, that the ould
Colonel got stricken in years, and he began to have misgivin's in his
conscience for his wicked doin's, and his heart was heavy as the fear
of death kem upon him; and sure enough, while he had such murnful
thoughts, the Divil kem to him, and towld him *he should go wid him.*

"Well, to be sure, the owld man was frekened, but he plucked up his courage and his cuteness, and towld the Divil, in a bantherin' way, jokin' like, that he had partic'lar business thin, that he was goin' to a party, and hoped an *owld friend* wouldn't inconvaynience him that a-way—"

"Well," said I, laughing at the "put off" of *going to a party*, "the Devil, of course, would take no excuse, and carried him off in a flash of fire?"

"Oh no, Sir," answered the old man, in something of a reproving, or, at least, offended tone—"that's the finish, I know very well, of many a story, such as we're talkin' of, but that's not the way of this, *which is thruth every word*, what I tell you —"

"I beg your pardon, for the interruption," said I.

"No offince in life, Sir," said the venerable chronicler, who was now deep in his story, and would not be stopped.

"Well, Sir," continued he, "the Divil said he'd call the next day, and that he must be ready; and sure enough, in the evenin', he kem to him; and when the Colonel seen him, he reminded him of his bargain, that as long as he could give him some work he couldn't do, he wasn't obleeged to go.

"'That's thrue,' says the Divil.

"'I'm glad you're as good as your word, anyhow,' says the Colonel.

"'I never bruk my word yit,' says the owld chap, cockin' up his horns consaitedly—'honor bright,' says he.

"'Well, then," says the Colonel, 'build me a mill, down there, by the river,' says he, 'and let me have it finished by tomorrow mornin'.'

"'Your will is my pleasure,' says the owld chap, and away he wint; and the Colonel thought he had nick'd Owld Nick at last, and wint to bed quite aasy in his mind.

"But, *jewel machree*, sure the first thing he heerd the next mornin' was that the whole counthry round was runnin' to see a fine bran new mill that was an the riverside, where, the evenin' before, not a thing at all, at all, but rushes was standin', and all, of coorse, wondherin' what brought it there; and some sayin' 'twas not lucky, and many more throubled in their mind, but one and all agreein' it was not *good*; and that's the very mill forninst you, that you were takin' aff, and the stone that I noticed is a remarkable one—a big coign-stone—that they say the Divil himself laid first, and has the mark of four fingers and a thumb on it, to this day.

"But when the Colonel heerd it, he was more throubled than any, of coorse, and began to conthrive what else he could think iv, to keep himself out of the claws of the *owld one*. Well, he often heerd tell that there was one thing the Divil never could do, and I dar say you heerd it too, Sir—that is, that he couldn't make a rope out of the sands of the sae; and so when the *owld one* kem to him the next day, and said his job was done, and that now the mill was built, he must either tell him somethin' else he wanted done, or come away wid him.

"So the Colonel said he saw it was all over wid him; 'but,' says he, 'I wouldn't like to go wid you alive, and sure it's all the same to you, alive or dead?'

"'Oh, that won't do," says his frind; 'I can't wait no more,' says he.

"'I don't want you to wait, my hear frind,' says the Colonel; 'all I want is, that you'll be plased to kill me, before you take me away."

"'With pleasure,' says Ould Nick.

"'But will you promise me my choice of dyin' one partic'lar way?' says the Colonel.

"'Half a dozen ways, if it plazes you,' says he.

"'You're mighty obleegin',' says the Colonel; 'and so,' says he, 'I'd rather die by bein' hanged with a rope *made out of the sands of the sae,*' says he, lookin' mighty knowin' at the *ould fellow*.

"'I've always one about me,' says the Divil, 'to obleege my frinds,' saye he; and with that, he pulls out a rope made of sand, sure enough.

"Oh, it's game you're makin',' says the Colonel, growin' as white as a sheet.

"'The game is mine, sure enough,' says the ould fellow, grinnin', with a terrible laugh.

"'That's not a sand-rope at all,' says the Colonel.

"'Isn't it?' says the Divil, hittin' him acrass the face with the ind iv the rope, and the sand (for it *was* made of sand, sure enough), the sand went into one of his eyes and made the tears come with the pain.

"'That bates all I ever seen or heerd,' says the Colonel, sthrivin' to rally, and make another offer—'is there anything you *can't* do?'

"'Nothin' you can tell me,' says the Divil, 'so you may as well lave off your palaverin', and come along at wanst.'

"'Will you give me one more offer?' says the Colonel.

"'You don't desarve it,' says the Divil, 'but I don't care if I do'; for you see, Sir, he was only playin' wid him, and tantalizing the ould sinner.

"'All fair,' says the Colonel, and with that, he ax'd him could he stop a woman's tongue?

"'Thry me,' says Ould Nick.

"'Well, then,' says the Colonel, 'make my lady's tongue be quiet for the next month, and I'll thank you.'

"'She'll never throuble you agin,' says Ould Nick; and, with that, the Colonel heerd roarin' and cryin', and the door of his room was threwn open, and in ran his daughter, and fell down at his feet, telling him her mother had just dhropped dead.

"The minit the door opened, the Divil runs and hides himself behind a big elbow-chair; and the Colonel was frekened almost out of his siven sinses, by raison of the sudden death of his poor lady, let alone the jeopardy he was in himself, seein' how the Divil had *forestall'd* him every way; and after ringin' his bell, and callin' in his sarvants, and recoverin' his daughther out of her faint, he was goin' away wid her o' the room, whin the Divil caught howld of him by the skirt of the coat, and the Colonel was obleeged to let his daughter be carried out by the sarvants, and shut the door afther them.

"'Well,' says the Divil, and he grinn'd and wagg'd his tail, all as one as a dog when he's plased—'what do you say now?' says he.

"'Oh,' says the Colonel, 'only lave me alone until I bury my poor wife,' says he, 'and I'll go with you then, you villain,' says he.

"'Don't call names,' says the Divil; 'you had betther keep a civil tongue in your head,' says he; 'and it doesn't become a gintleman to forget good manners.'

"Well, Sir, to make a long story short, the Divil purtended to let him off, out of kindness, for three days, antil his wife was buried; but the raison of it was this, that when the lady his daughther fainted, he loosened the clothes about her throat, and in pulling some of her dhress away, he tuk off a goold chain that was an her neck, and put it in his pocket, and the chain had a diamond crass an it, (the Lord be praiscd!) and the Divil darn't touch him while he had the *sign of the crass* about him.

"Well, the poor Colonel, God forgive him, was grieved for the loss of his lady, and she had an *iligant berrin*—and they say, that when the prayers was readin' over the dead, the ould Colonel took it to heart like anything, and the word o' God kem home to his poor sinful sowl at last.

"Well, Sir, to make a long story short, the ind iv it was, that for the three days o' grace that was given to him, the poor deluded ould sinner did nothin' at all but read the Bible from mornin' till night, and bit or sup didn't pass his lips all the time, he was so intint upon the holy book, but sat up in an ould room in the far ind iv the house, and bid no one disturb him an no account, and struv to make his heart bould with the words iv life; and sure it was somethin' strinthened him at last, though as the time drew nigh that the *inimy* was to come, he didn't feel aisy,—and no wondher; and, by dad, the three days was past and gone in no time, and the story goes, that at the dead hour o' the night, when the poor sinner was readin' away as fast as he could, my jew'l, his heart jumped up to his mouth, at gettin' a tap on the shouldher.

"'Oh, murther!' says he, 'who's there?' for he was afraid to look up.

"'I'ts me,' says the *ould one*, and he stood right foreninst him, and his eyes like coals o' fire, lookin' him through, and he said, with a voice that a'most split his ould heart, 'Come!' says he.

"'Another day,' cried out the poor Colonel.

"'Not another hour,' says Sat'n.

"'Half an hour?'

"'Not a quarther,' says the Divil, grinnin', with a bitther laugh— 'give over your readin', I bid you,' says he, 'and come away wid me.'

"'Only gi' me a few minutes' says he.

"'Lave off your palaverin', you sneakin' ould sinner,' says Sat'n; 'you know you're bought and sould to me, and a purty bargain I have o' you, you ould baste,' says he—'so come along at wanst,' and he put out his claw to ketch him; but the Colonel tuk a fast hould o' the Bible, and begg'd hard that he'd let him alone, and wouldn't harm him antil the bit o' candle that was just blinkin' in the socket before him, was burned out.

"'Well, have it so, you dirty coward,' says Ould Nick, and with that he spit an him.

"But the poor ould Colonel didn't lose a minit, (for he was cunnin' to the ind,) but snatched the little taste o'candle that was foreninst him, out 'o the candlestick, and puttin' it an the holy book before him, he shut down the cover an it, and quinched the light. With that, the Divil gave a roar like a bull, and vanished in a flash o' fire, and the poor Colonel fainted away in his chair; but the sarvants heerd the noise, (for the Divil tore aff the roof o' the house when he left it,) and run into the room, and brought their master to himself agin. And from that day out he was an althered man, and used to have the Bible read to him every day, for he couldn't read himself any more, by raison of losin' his eyesight, when the Divil hit him with the rope of sand in the face, and afther, spit an him—for the sand wint into one eye, and he lost the other that-a-way, savin' your presence.

"So you see, Sir, afther all, the Colonel, undher heaven, was too able for the Divil, and by readin' the good book, his sowl was saved, and (Glory be to God) *isn't that mighty improvin'?*"

Darby Doyle's
Voyage to Quebec
From *Dublin Penny Journal*

I TUCK the road, one fine morning in May, from Inchegelagh, an' got up to the Cove safe an' sound. There I saw many ships with big broad boords fastened to ropes, everyone ov them saying, "The first vessel for Quebec." Siz I to myself, "Those are about to run for a wager; this one siz she'll be first." At any rate, I pitched on one that was finely painted, and looked long and slender like a corragh on the Shannon. When I wint on board to ax the fare, who shou'd come up out ov a hole but Ned Finn, an ould townsman ov my own. "Och, is it yoor-self that's there, Ned?" siz I; "are ye goin' to Amerrykey?" "Why, an' to be sure," siz he; "I'm *mate* ov the ship." "Meat! that's yer sort, Ned," siz I; "then we'll only want bread. Hadn't I better go and pay my way?" "You're time enough," siz Ned; "I'll tell you when we're ready for sea —leave the rest to me, Darby." "Och, tip us your fist," siz I; "you were always the broath ov a boy; for the sake ov ould times, Ned, we must have a dhrop." So, my jewel, Ned brought me to where there was right good stuff. When it got up to three o'clock I found myself mighty weak with hunger. I got the smell ov corn beef an' cabbage that knock'd me up entirely. I then wint to the landleddy, and siz I to her, "Maybee your leddyship id not think me rood by axin' iv Ned an myself cou'd get our dinner ov that fine hot mate that I got a taste ov in my nose?" "In troath you can," siz she (an' she look'd mighty pleasant), "an' welkim," So, my darlin' dish and all came up. "That's what I call a *flaugholoch* mess," siz I. So we ate and drank away. Many's the squeeze Ned gave my fist, telling me to leave it all to him, and how comfortable he'd make me on the voyage. Day after day we spint together, waitin' for the wind, till I found my pockets begin to grow very light. At last, siz he to me, one day after dinner, "Darby, the ship will be ready for sea on the morrow—you'd betther be on boord, an' pay your way." "Is it jokin' you are, Ned?" siz I; "shure you tould me to leave it all to you." "Ah! Darby," siz he, "you're for takin' a rise out o' me; shure enough, ye were the lad that was never without a joke—the very priest himself couldn't get over ye. But, Darby, there's no joke like the thrue one. I'll stick to my promise; hut, Darby, you must pay your way." "O Ned," siz 1, "is this the way you're goin' to threat me afther all? I'm a rooin'd man; all I cou'd scrape together I spint on you. If you don't do something for me, I'm lost. Is there no place where you cou'd hide me from the captin?" "Not a place," siz Ned. "An' where, Ned, is the place I saw you comin' out ov?" "Oh, Darby, that was the hould where the cargo's stow'd." "An' is there no other place?" siz I. "Oh,. yes," siz he, "where we keep the wather casks." "An', Ned," siz I, "does anyone live down there?" "Not a mother's soul," siz he. "An', Ned," siz I, "can't you cram me down there, and give me a lock ov straw an' a bit?" "Why, Darby," siz he (an' he look'd mighty pittyfull). "I must thry. But mind, Darby, you'll have to hide all day in an empty barrel, an' when it comes to my watch, I'll bring you down some grog; but if you're diskiver'd, it's all over with me, an' you'll be put on a dissilute island to starve." "O Ned," siz I, "leave it all to me." "Never fear, Darby, I'll mind my eye." When night cum on I got down into the dark cellar, among the barrels; poor Ned fixt a place in a corner for me to sleep, an' every night he brought me down hard black cakes an' salt meat. There I lay snug for a whole month. At last, one night, siz he to me, "Now, Darby, what's to be done? we're within three days' sail of Quebec; the ship will be overhauled, and all the passengers' names call'd over; if you are found, you'll be sould as a slave for your passage money." "An' is that all that frets you, my jewel," siz I; "can't you leave it all to me? In throath, Ned, I'll never forget your hospitality at any rate. But, what place is outside of the ship?" "Why, the sea, to be sure," siz he. "Och! botheration," siz I, "I mean what's the outside the ship?" "Why, Darby," siz he, "part of it's called the bulwark." "An' fire an' faggots," siz I, "is it bulls work the vessel along?" "No, nor horses," siz he, "neither; this is no time for jokin'; what do you mean to do?" "Why, I'll tell you, Ned; get me an empty meal-bag, a bottle, an' a bare ham-bone, and that's all I'll ax." So, begad, Ned look'd very queer at me; so he got them for me, anyhow. "Well, Ned," siz I, "you know I'm a great shwimmer; your watch will be early in the mornin'; I'll jist slip down into the sea; do you cry out, there's a man in the wather, as loud as you can, and leave all the rest to me."

Well, to be sure, down into the sea I dropt without so much as a splash. Ned roared out with the hoarseness of a brayin' ass—"a man in the sea! a man in the sea!" every man, woman, and child came running up out of the holes, the captin among the rest, who put a long red barrel like a gun to his eye—gibbet me, but I thought he was for shootin' me! down I dived. When I got my head over the wather agen, what shou'd I see but a boat rowin' to me, as fast as a throut afther a pinkeen. When it came up close enough to be heard, I roared out: "Bad end to yees, for a set ov spalpeen rascals, did ye hear me at last?" The boat now run 'pon the top ov me; down I dived agen like a duck afther a frog, but the minnit my skull came over the wather, I was gript by the scruff ov the neck, and dhragged into the boat. To be shure, I didn't kick up a row—"Let go my hair, ye blue devils," I roared, "it's well ye have me in your marcy in this dissilute place, or by the powthers I'd make ye feel the strinth ov my bones. What hard look I had to follow yees, at all at all—which ov ye is the masther?" As I sed this every mother's son began to stare at me, with my bag round my neck, an' my bottle by my side, an' the bare bone in my fist. "There he is," siz they, pointin' to a little yellow man in a corner of the boat. "May the—rise blisthers on your rapin'-hook shins," siz I, "you yallow-lookin' monkey, but it's a'most time for you to think ov lettin' me into your ship I'm here plowin' and plungin' this month afther ye; shure I didn't care a thrawneen was it not that you have my best Sunday clothes in your ship, and my name in your books. For three sthraws, if I don't know how to write, I'd leave my mark, an' that on your skull"; so saying I made a lick at him with the ham-bone, but I was near tumblin' into the sea agen. "An', pray, what is your name, my lad?" siz the captin. "What's my name! What id you give to know?" siz I, "ye unmannerly spalpeen, it might be what's your name, Darby Doyle, out ov your mouth—ay, Darby Doyle, that was never afraid or ashamed to own it at home or abroad!" "An', Mr. Darby Doyle," siz he, "do you mean to persuade us that you swum from Cork to this afther us?" "This is more ov your ignorance," siz I—"ay, an' if you sted three days longer and not take me up, I'd be in Quebec before ye, only my purvisions werc out, and the few rags ov bank notes I had all melted into paste in my pocket, for I hadn't time to get them changed. But stay, wait till I get my foot on shore; there's ne'er a cottoner in Cork iv you don't pay for leavin' me to the marcy ov the waves."

All this time the blue chaps were pushin' the boat with sticks through the wather, till at last we came close to the ship. Everyone on board saw me at the Cove, but didn't see me on the voyage; to be sure, everyone's mouth was wide open, crying out Darby Doyle. "The— stop your throats," siz I, "it's now you call me loud enough, ye wouldn't shout that way when ye saw me rowlin' like a tub in a millrace the other day fornenst your faces." When they heard me say that, some of them grew pale as a sheet— every thumb was at work till they a'most brought the blood from their forreds. But, my jewel, the captin does no more than runs to the book an' calls out the names that paid, and them that wasn't paid—to be shure, I was one ov them that didn't pay. If the captin looked at me before with wondherment, he now looked with astonishment! Nothin' was tawk'd ov for the other three days but Darby Doyle's great shwim from the Cove to Quebec. One sed, "I always knew Darby to be a great schwimmer." "Do ye remimber," siz another, "when Darby's dog was nigh been drownded in the great duck hunt, when Darby peeled off and brought in the dog, and made afther the duck himself, and swum for two hours endways; and do ye remimber when all the dogs gother round the duck at one time; whin it wint down how Darby dived afther it, and sted down for a'most an hour—and sted below while the creathur was eatin' a few frogs, for she was weak an' hungry; and when everybody thought he was lost, up he came with the duck by the leg in his kithogue [left hand]."   Begar, I agreed to all they sed, till at last we got to Amerrykey. I was now in a quare way; the captain wouldn't let me go till a friend of his would see me. By this time, my jewel, not only his friends came, but swarms upon swarms, starin' at poor Darby. At last I called Ned. "Ned, avic," siz I, "I want to go about my *bisness.*" "Be easy, Darby," siz he; "haven't ye your fill ov good aitin'", an' the Captain's got mighty fond ov ye entirely." "Is he, Ned?" siz I; "but tell us, Ned, are all them crowds ov people goin' to sea?" "Augh, ye omadham," siz Ned, "sure they are come to look at you." Just as he said this, a tall yellow man, with a black curly head, comes and stares me full in the face. "You'll know me agen," says I, "bad luck to yer manners and the schoolmasther that taught ye." But I thought he was goin' to shake hands with me, when he tuck hould ov my fist and opencd every finger, one by one, then opened my shirt and look't at my breast. "Pull away, mabouchal," siz I, "I'm no desarthur, at any rate." But never an answer he made, but walk'd down into the hole where the captin lived. "This is more ov it," siz I; "Ned, what cou'd that tallah-faced man mean?" "Why," siz Ned, "he was lookin' to see iv your fingers were webb'd, or had ye scales on your breast." "His impidence is great," siz I; "did he take me for a duck or a bream? But, Ned, what's the meanin' ov the boords acrass the stick the people walk on, and the big white boord up there?" "Why, come over and read," siz Ned. But, my jewel, I didn't know whether I was stannin' on my head or on my heels when I saw in great big black letters:

THE GREATEST WONDHER OF THE: WORLD
TO BE SEEN HERE,
A Man that beats out Nicholas the Divel!
He has swum from Cork to Amerrykey! !
Proved on oath by ten of the Crew and twenty Passengers.
Admittance Half a Dollar.

"Bloody wars! Ned," siz I, "does this mean your humble sarvint?" "Divil another," siz he,—so I makes no more ado, than with a hop, skip, and jump, gets over to the captin, who was now talkin' to the yellow fellow that was afther starin' me out ov countenance. "Pardon my rudeness, your honor," siz I, mighty polite, and makin' a bow—at the same time Ned was at my heels—so rising my foot to give the genteel scrape, sure I scraped all the skin off Ned's shins. "May bad luck to your brogues," siz he. "You'd betther not curse the wearer," siz I, "or—" "Oh, Darby!" siz the captin, "don't be unginteel, an' so many ladies and gintlemin lookin' at ye." "The never another mother's soul shall lay their peepers on me till 1 see sweet Inchegelagh agen," says I. "Begar ye are doin' it well. How much money have ye gother for my shwimmin'?" "Be quiet, Darby," siz the captin, and he looked very much friekened. "I have plenty, an' I'll have more for ye iv ye do what I want ye to do." "An' what is it, avic?" siz I. "Why, Darby," siz he, "I'm afther houldin' a wager last night with this gintleman for all the worth ov my ship, that you'll shwim against any shwimmer in the world; an', Darby, if ye don't do that, I'm a gone man." "Augh, give us your fist," siz I; "did ye ever hear ov Paddys dishaving any man in the European world yet—barrin' themselves?" "Well, Darby," siz he, "I'll give you a hundred dollars; but, Darby, you must be to your word, and you shall have another hundred." So sayin', he brought me down into the cellar; but, my jewel, I didn't think for the life ov me to see such a wondherful place—nothin' bul goold every way I turned, and Darby's own sweet face in twenty places. Begar I was a'most ashamed to ax the gintleman for the dollars. "But," siz I to myself agen, "the gintleman has too much money, I suppose he does be throwin' it into the sea, for I often heard the sea was richer than the land, so I may as well take it anyhow." "Now, Darby," siz he, "here's the dollars for ye." But, begar, it was only a bit of paper he was handin' me. "Arrah, none ov yer tricks upon thravelers," siz I; "I had betther nor that, and many more ov them, melted in the sea; give me what won't wash out ov my pocket." "Why, Darby," siz he, "this is an ordher on a marchant for the amount." "Pho, pho!" siz I, "I'd sooner take your word nor his oath"—lookin' round mighty respectful at the goold walls. "Well, Darby," siz he, "ye must have the real thing." So, by the powthers, he reckon'd me out a hundred dollars in goold. I never saw the like since the stockin' fell out of the chimly on my aunt and cut her forred. "Now, Darby," siz he, "ye are a rich man, an' ye are worthy of it all—sit down, Darby, an' take a bottle ov wine." So to please the gintleman, I sat down. Afther a bit, who comes down but Ned. "Captin," siz he, "the deck is crowded; I had to block up the gangway to prevint anymore from comin' in to see Darby. Bring him up, or, blow me, iv the ship won't be sunk." "Come up, Darby," siz the captin', lookin' roguish pleasant at myself. So, my jewel, he handed me up through the hall as tendher as iv I was a lady, or a pound ov fresh butther in the dog days. When I got up, shure enough, I couldn't help starin'; such crowds of fine ladies and yallow gintlemen never was seen before in any ship. One ov them, a little rosy-cheek'd beauty, whispered the captin somethin', but he shuk his head, and then came over to me. "Darby," siz he, "I know an Irishman would do anything to please a lady." "In throth you may say that with yer own ugly mouth," siz I. "Well, then, Darby," siz he, "the ladies would wish to see you give a few strokes in the sea." "Och, an' they shall have them in welcome," siz I. "That's a good fellow," siz he; "now strip off."

"Decency, Katty," siz I; "is it in my mother-naked pelt before the ladies? Bad luck to the undacent brazen-faced—but no matther! Irish girls forever, afther all!" But all to no use. I was made to peel off behind a big sheet, and then I made one race and jumpt ten yards into the wather to get out ov their sight. Shure enough, everyone's eyes danced in their head, while they look'd on the spot where I went down. A thought came into my head while I was below, how I'd show them a little divarsion, as I could use a great many thricks on the wather. So I didn't rise at all till I got to the tother side, and everyone run to that side; then I took a hoult ov my big two toes, and makin' a ring ov myself, rowled like a hoop on the top ov the wather all round the ship. I b'leeve I opened their eyes! Then I yarded, back-swum, an' dived, till at last the captin made signs for me to come out, so I got into the boat an' threw on my duds. The very ladies were breakin' their necks runnin' to shake hands with me. "Shure," siz they, "you're the greatest man in the world!!" So for three days I showed off to crowds ov people, though I was fryin' in the wather for shame. At last the day came that I was to stand the tug. I saw the captin lookin' very often at me. At last, "Darby," siz he, "are you any way cow'd? The fellow you have to shwim agenst can shwim down watherfalls an' catharacts." "Can, he, avic?" siz I; "but can he shwim up agenst them? Wow, wow, Darby, for that! But, captin, come here; is all my purvisions ready?— don't let me fall short ov a dhrop ov the rale stuff above all things." An' who shou'd come up while I was tawkin' to the captin but the chap I was to shwim with, an' heard all I sed. Begad! his eyes grew as big as two oysther shells. Then the captin call'd me aside. "Darby," siz he, "do ye put on this green jacket an' white throwsers, that the people may bether extinguish you from the other chap." "With all hearts, avic," siz I, "green forever—Darby's own favorite color the world over; but where am I goin' to, captain?" "To the shwimmin' place, to be shure," siz he. "Divil shoot the failers an' take the hindmost," siz I; "here's at ye." I was then inthrojuiced to the shwimmer. I look'd at him from head to foot. He was so tall that he could eat bread an' butther over my head—with a face as yallow as a kite's foot. "Tip us the mitten," siz I, "mabouchal," siz I. (But, begad, I was puzzled. "Begar," siz I to myself, "I'm done. Cheer up, Darby! If I'm not able to kill him, I'll frighten the life out ov him.") "Where are we goin' to shwim to?" But never a word he answered. "Are ye bothered, neighbor?" "I reckon I'm not," siz he, mighty chuff. "Well, then," siz I, "why didn't ye answer your betthers? What id ye think iv we shwum to Keep Cleer or the Keep ov Good Hope?" "I reckon neither," siz he agen, eyein' me as iv I was goin' to pick his pockets. "Well, then, have ye any favorite place?" siz I. "Now, I've heard a great deal about the place where poor Boney died; I'd like to see it, iv I'd anyone to show me the place; suppose we wint there?" Not a taste of a word cou'd I get out ov him, good or bad. Off we set through the crowds ov ladies an' ginllemen. Such cheerin' and wavin' ov hats was never seen even at *Dan's* enthry; an' then the row ov purty girls laughin' an' rubbin' up against me, that I could har'ly get on. To be shure, no one cou'd be lookin' to the ground, an' not be lookin' at them, till at last I was thript up by a big loomp ov iron stuck fast in the ground with a big ring to it. "Whoo, Darby!" siz I, makin' a hop an' a crack ov my fingers, "you're not down yet." I turn'd roun' to look at what thript me. "What d'ye call that?" siz I to the captin, who was at my elbow. "Why, Darby?" siz he; "that's half an anchor." "Have ye any use for it?" siz I. "Not in the least," siz he; "it's only to fasten boats to." "Maybee, you'd give it to a body," siz I. "An' welkim, Darby," siz he; "it's yours." "God bless your honor, sir," siz I, "it's my poor father that will pray for you. When I left home the creather hadn't as much as an anvil but what was sthreeled away by the agint—bad end to them. This will be jist the thing that'll match him; he can tie the horse to the ring, while he forges on the other part. Now, will ye obleege me by gettin' a couple ov chaps to lay it on my shoulder when I get into the wather, and I won't have to be comin back for it afther I shake hans with this fellow." Begar, the chap turned from yallow to white when he heard me say this. An' siz he to the gintleman that was walkin' by *his* side, "I reckon I'm not fit for the shwimmin' today—I don't feel *myself*." "An', murdher an Irish, if you're yer brother, can't you send him for yerself, an' I'll wait here till he comes. Here, man, take a dhrop ov this before ye go. Here's to yer betther health, and your brother's info the bargain." So I took off my glass, and handed him another; but the never a dhrop ov it he'd take. "No force," siz I, "avic; maybe you think there's poison in it—well, here's another good luck to us. An' when will ye be able for the shwim, avic?" siz I, mighty complisant. "I reckon in another week," siz he. So we shook hands and parted. The poor fellow went home—took the fever—then began to rave. "Shwim up the catharacts!—shwim to the Keep ov Good Hope!—shwim to St. Helena!—shwim to Keep Cleer!—shwim with an anchor on his back! —Oh! oh! oh!"

I now thought it best to be on the move; so I gother up my winners; and here I sit undher my own hickory threes, as independent as any Yankee.

Index